The 1960s

ISBN 0-634-04059-6

HAL•LEONARD® CORPORATION

7777 W. BLUEMOUND RD. P.O. BOX 13819 MILWAUKEE, WI 53213

Visit Hal Leonard Online at
www.halleonard.com

CONTENTS

Badge

Words and Music by Eric Clapton and George Harrison

Guitar Solo

Gtr. 2: w/ Rhy. Fig. 2, 3 1/4 times, simile
Gtr. 1: w/ Rhy. Fig. 3, 3 1/4 times, simile

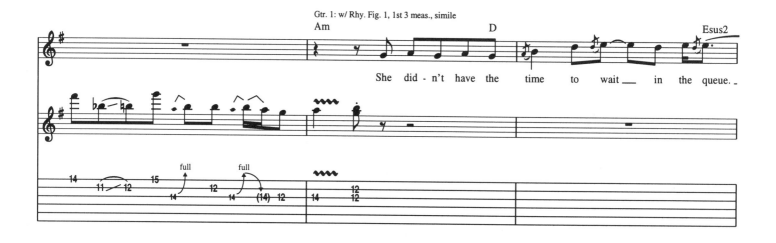

Gtr. 1: w/ Rhy. Fig. 1, 1st 3 meas., simile

She did-n't have the time to wait __ in the queue. __

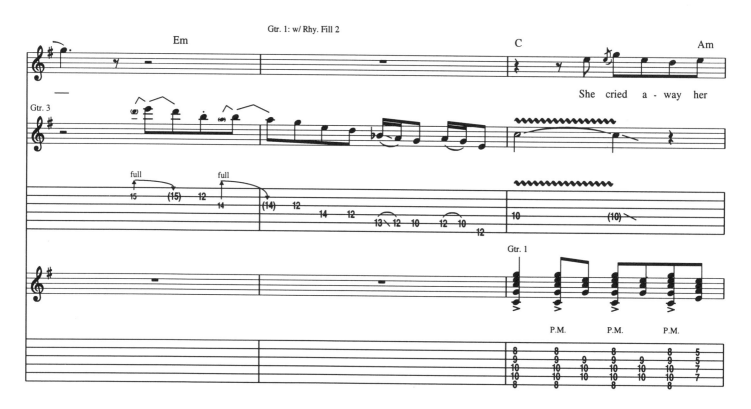

Gtr. 1: w/ Rhy. Fill 2

She cried a - way her

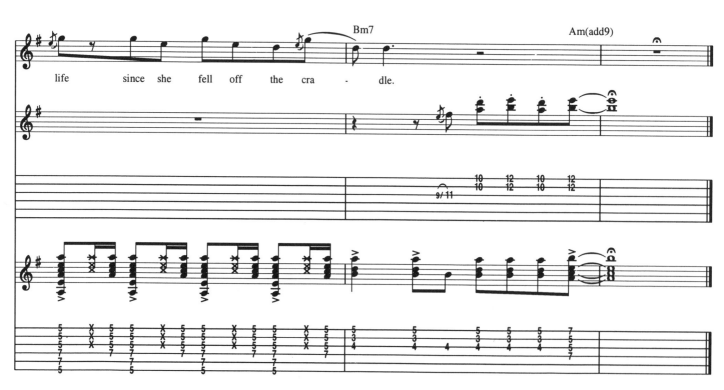

life since she fell off the cra - dle.

Blackbird

Words and Music by John Lennon and Paul McCartney

*Strum upstemmed notes w/ index fin. of pick hand
whenever more than one upstemmed note appears.

ment to a - rise. ___

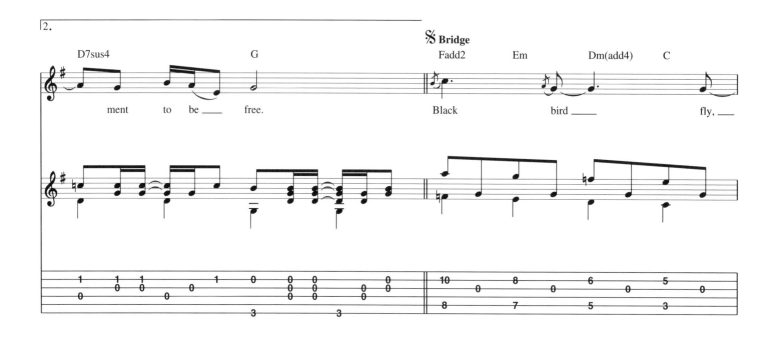

ment to be ___ free.

Bridge

Black bird ___ fly, ___

black bird ___ fly ___

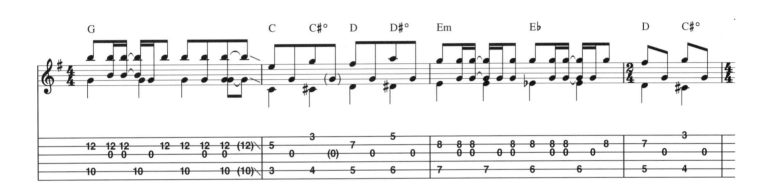

D.S. al Coda 1

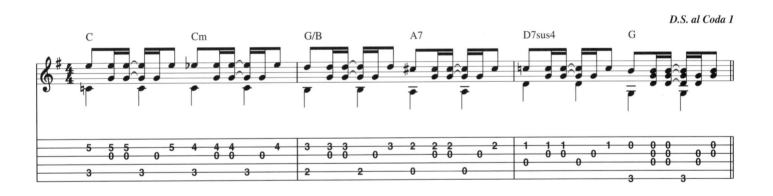

⊕ Coda 1

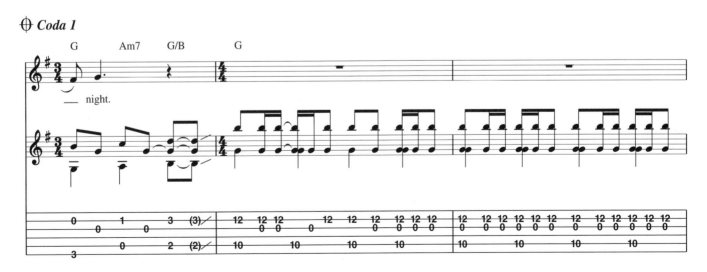

 ⊕ *Coda 2*

you were on - ly wait - ing for this mo - ment to a - rise. ___

You were on - ly ___ wait-ing for this mo - ment to a - rise. ___

You were on - ly wait-ing ___ for this mo - ment to a - rise. ___

Fun, Fun, Fun

Words and Music by Brian Wilson and Mike Love

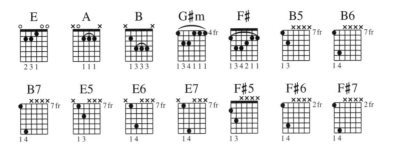

Tune down 1/2 step:
(low to high) Eb–Ab–Db–Gb–Bb–Eb

Intro

Moderately fast ♩ = 168

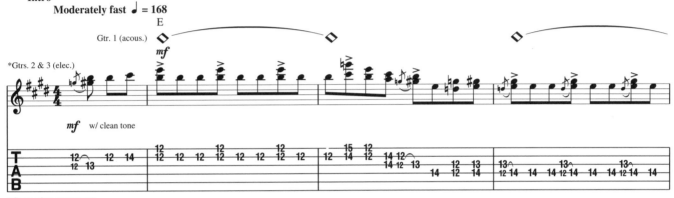

*Composite arrangement

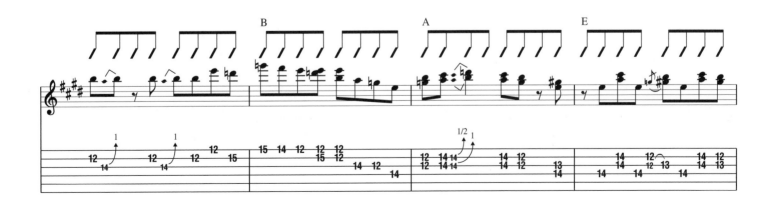

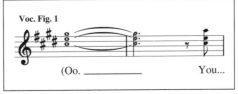

In - dy Five Hun - dred look like ___ a Ro - man char - i - ot race, ___ now.
Oo. ___ You look like an ace, ___ now, you

look like an ace. ___
A lot - ta guys try to catch her but she leads them on a wild goose chase, ___
Oo. ___ You

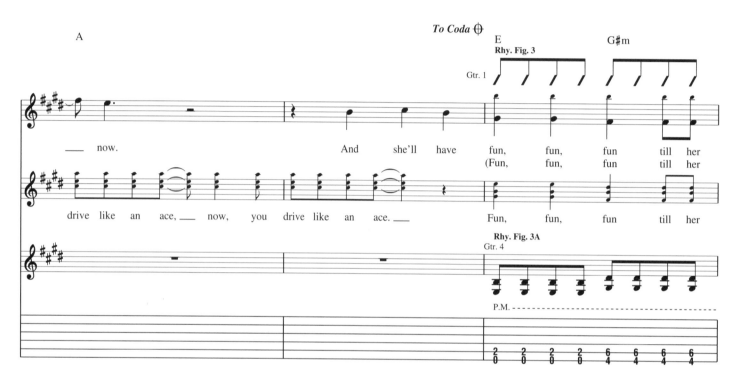

___ now.
And she'll have fun, fun, fun till her
(Fun, fun, fun till her

drive like an ace, ___ now, you drive like an ace. ___
Fun, fun, fun till her

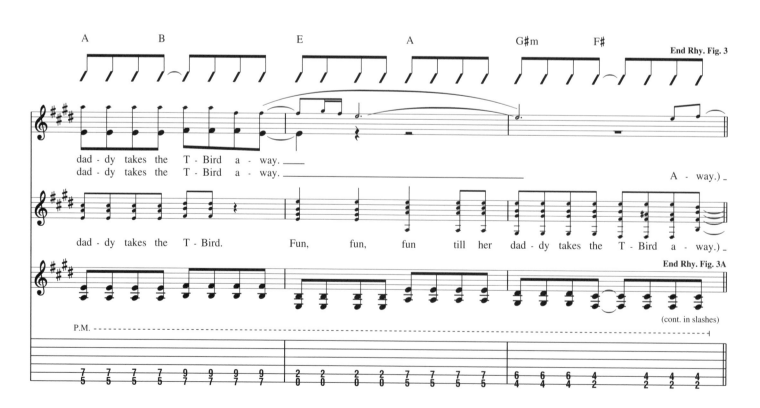

dad - dy takes the T - Bird a - way. ___
dad - dy takes the T - Bird a - way. ___
A - way.)

dad - dy takes the T - Bird.
Fun, fun, fun till her dad - dy takes the T - Bird a - way.)

Guitar Solo

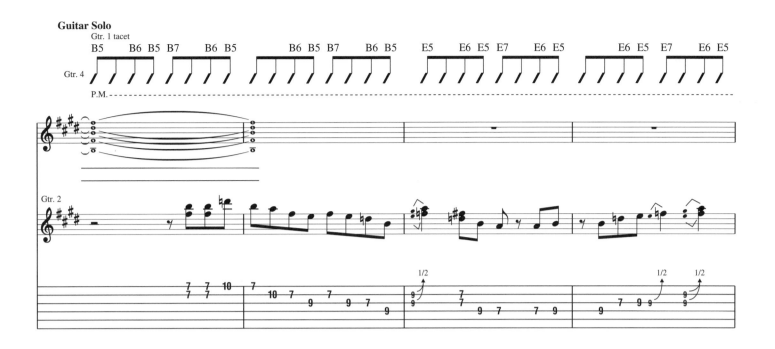

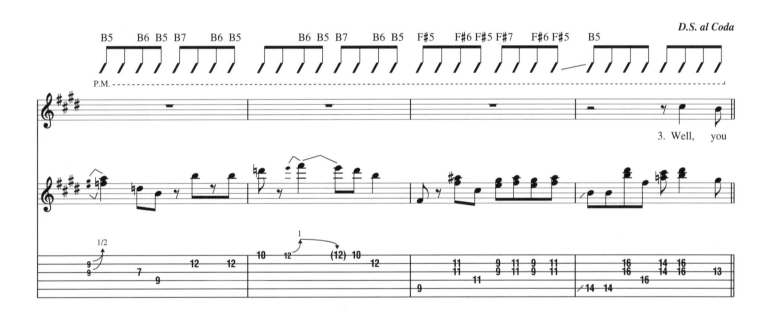

D.S. al Coda

⊕ **Coda**

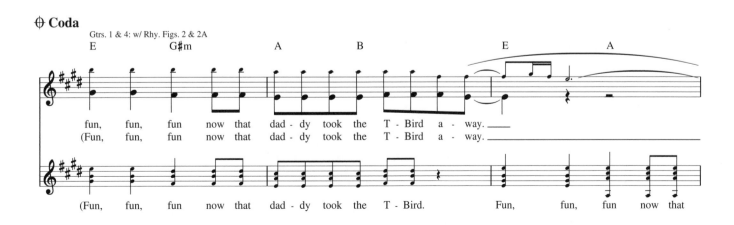

Additional Lyrics

Well, you knew all along
That your dad was gettin' wise to you, now.
(You shouldn't have lied, now, you shouldn't have lied.)
And since he took your set of keys
You've been thinkin' that your fun is all through, now.
(You shouldn't have lied, now, you shouldn't have lied.)
But you can come along with me
'Cause we got a lotta things to do now.
(You shouldn't have lied, now, you shouldn't have lied.)
And we'll...

Gloria

Words and Music by Van Morrison

Good Lovin'

Words and Music by Rudy Clark and Arthur Resnick

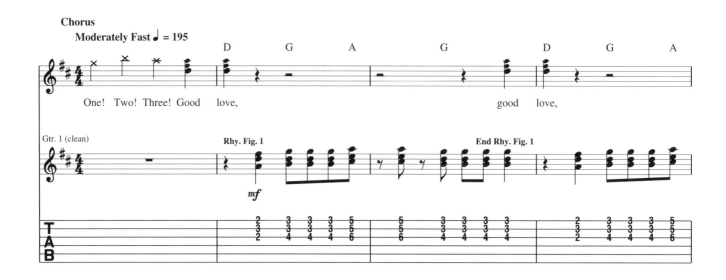

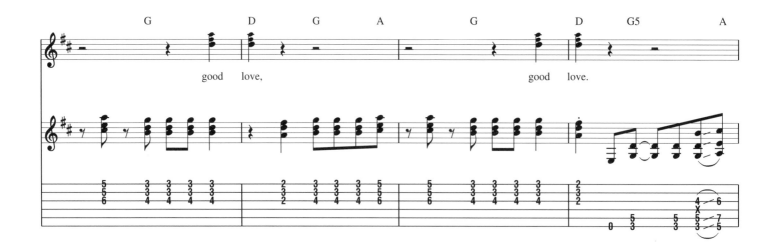

Verse

Gtr. 1: w/ Rhy. Fig. 1 (8 times)

-in' so ___ bad. ___ I

asked my fam - 'ly doc - tor just what I had. ___ I ___ said,

"Doc - tor, now can you tell ___
(Doc - tor.) ___ Mis - ter M. D., (Doc - tor.) ___

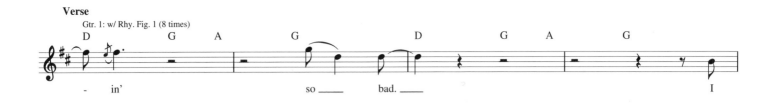

___ me what's ail - in' me?" He ___ said,
(Doc - tor.) ___

"Yeah, yeah, ___ yeah, ___ yeah, yeah." Yes in -
(Yeah, yeah, ___ yeah, ___ yeah, yeah.)

Gtr. 1

Pre-Chorus

deed, all I, I real - ly need. ___
(Good

let ring

Chorus

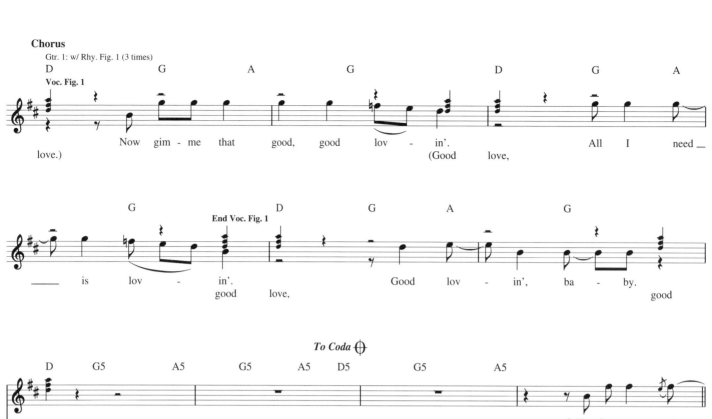

To Coda ⊕

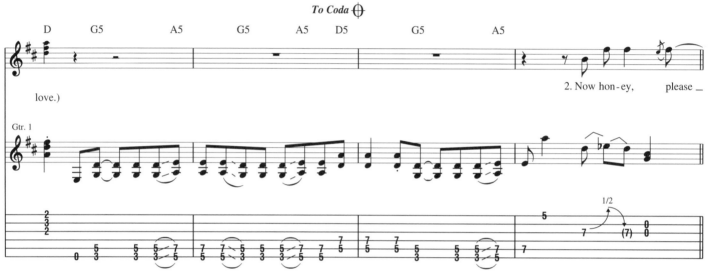

Verse

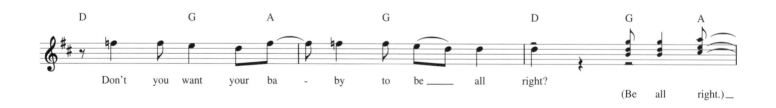

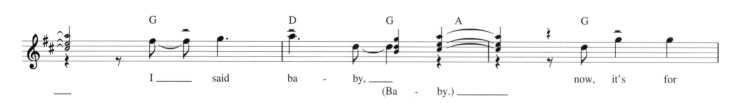

sure.

(It's   for   sure.) ____

I ____ got   the   fev - er,   yeah, ____

D.S. al Coda

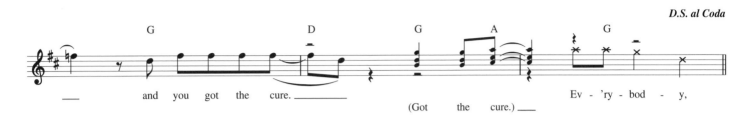

____   and   you   got   the   cure. ____

(Got   the   cure.) ____

Ev - 'ry - bod - y,

⊕ Coda

Organ Solo

Gtr. 1: w/ Rhy. Fig. 1 (7 times)

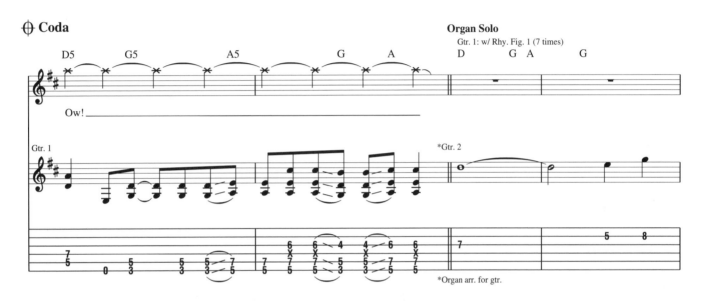

Ow! ____

Gtr. 1

*Gtr. 2

*Organ arr. for gtr.

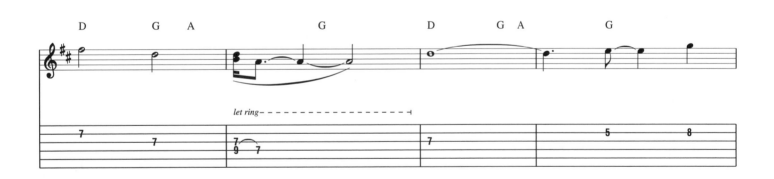

let ring - - - - - - - - - - - - -

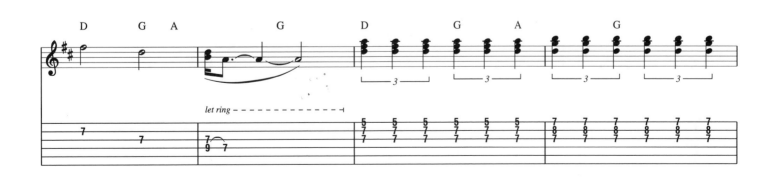

let ring - - - - - - - - - - - - -

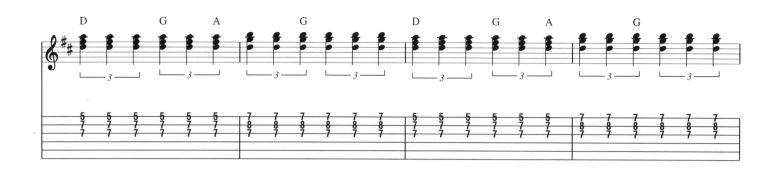

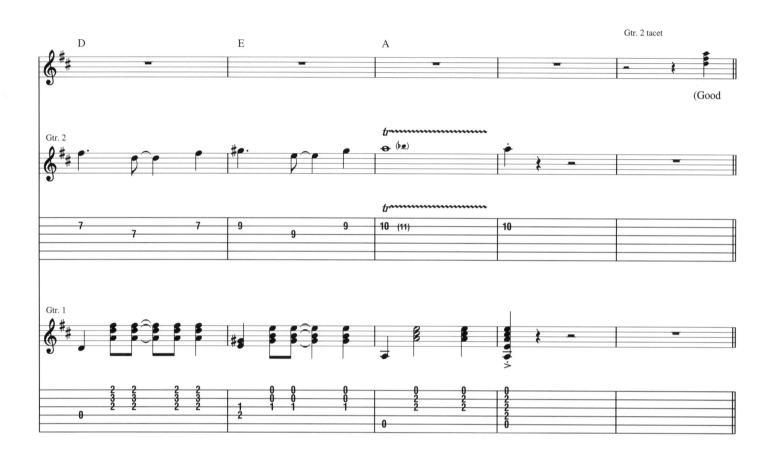

(Good

Chorus

Lead Voc.: w/ ad. Lib. (next 16 meas.)
Bkgd. Voc.: w/ Voc. Fig. 1 (3 3/4 times)
Gtr. 1: w/ Rhy. Fig. 1 (8 times)

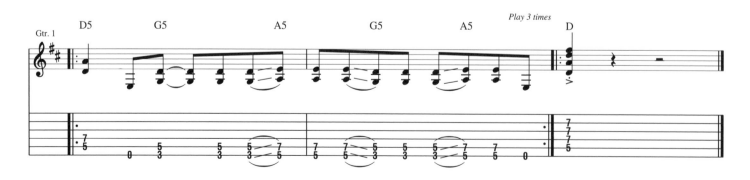

Green Onions

Written by Al Jackson, Jr., Lewis Steinberg, Booker T. Jones and Steve Cropper

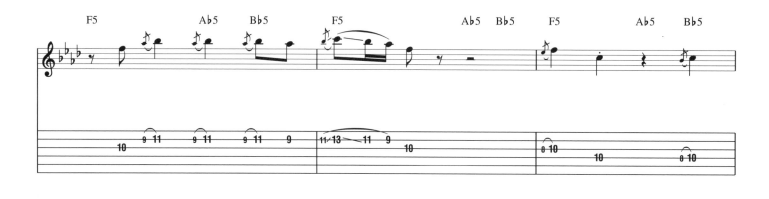

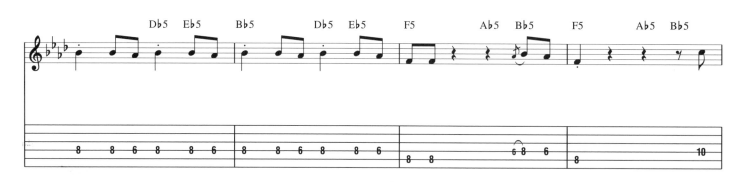

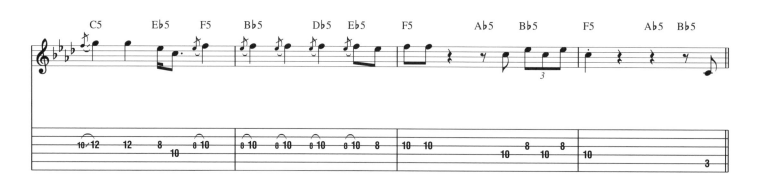

F **Outro**

Gtr. 1: w/ Rhy. Fig. 1 (5 times)

Gtr. 2

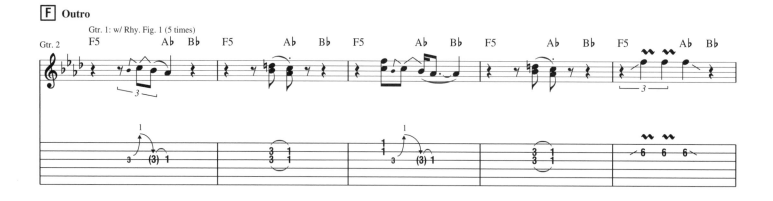

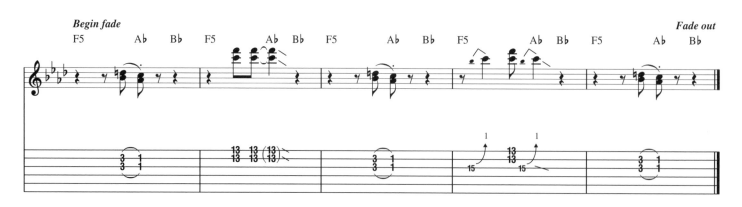

Happy Together

Words and Music by Garry Bonner and Alan Gordon

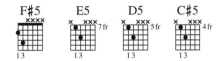

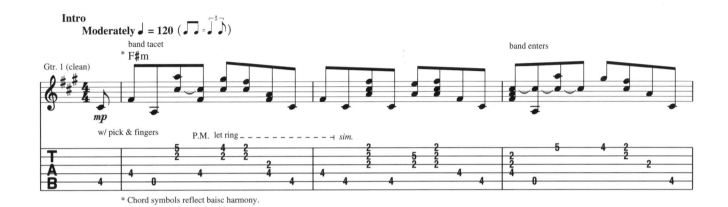

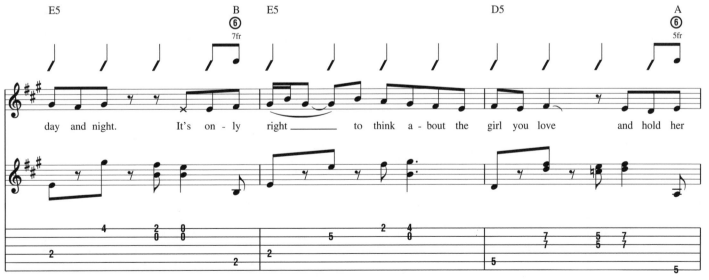

ba - by the skies ___ will be blue for all my ___ life. _____

End Rhy. Fig. 2

Verse

Gtrs. 1 & 2: w/ Rhy. Figs. 1 & 1A, simile

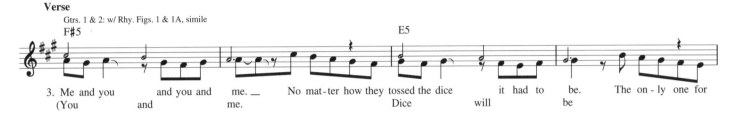

3. Me and you ___ and you and ___ me. ___ No mat-ter how they tossed the dice ___ it had to ___ be. The on - ly one for
(You ___ and ___ me. ___ Dice ___ will ___ be

D.S. al Coda

Gtrs. 1 & 2: w/ Rhy. Fill 1, simile

me is you ___ and you for ___ me. ___ So hap - py ___ to ___ geth - er. _____
You ___ for ___ me.)

⊕ *Coda*

Verse

Gtrs. 1 & 2: w/ Rhy. Figs. 1 & 1A, simile

4. Me and you ___ and you and ___ me. ___ No mat - ter how they tossed the dice ___ it had to

be. The on - ly one for me is you ___ and you for ___ me. ___ So hap - py ___ to ___ geth - er. _____

Interlude

Gtrs. 1 & 2: w/ Rhy. Fill 1, simile ___ Gtrs. 1 & 2: w/ Rhy. Fig. 2, simile

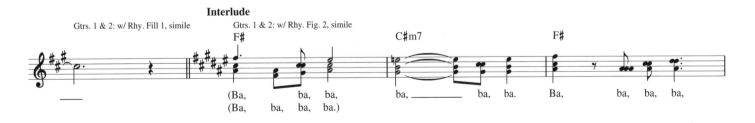

___ (Ba, ___ ba, ba, ___ ba, ___ ba, ba. Ba, ___ ba, ba, ba,
(Ba, ___ ba, ba, ba.)

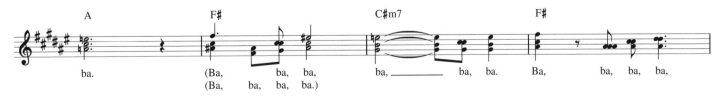

ba. ___ (Ba, ___ ba, ba, ___ ba, ___ ba, ba. Ba, ___ ba, ba, ba,
(Ba, ___ ba, ba, ba.)

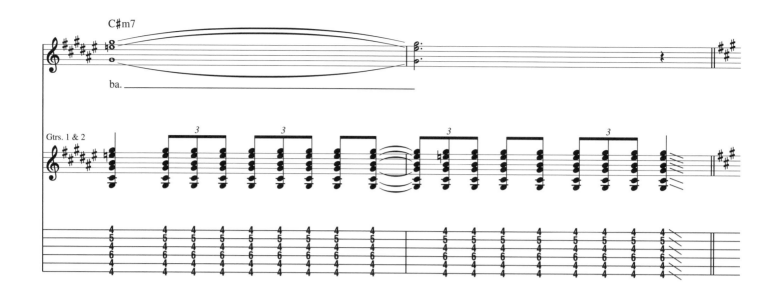

Verse
Gtrs. 1 & 2: w/ Rhy. Figs. 1 & 1A, 1st 6 meas., simile

5. Me and you and you and me. __ No mat-ter how they tossed the dice it had to
(Ah. __   Ah. __

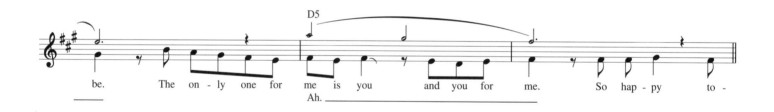

be. The on-ly one for me is you and you for me. So hap-py to-
Ah. __

Outro

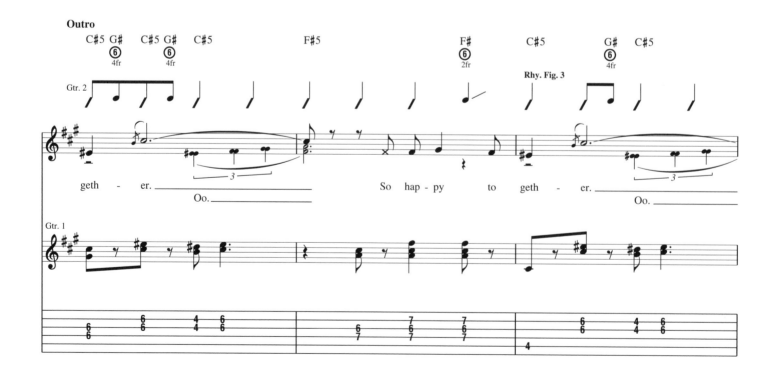

geth - er. __ So hap-py to geth - er. __
Oo. __   Oo. __

Hello Mary Lou

Words and Music by Gene Pitney and C. Mangiaracina

Ma - ry Lou __ I'm so __ in love __ with you. __ I —

*Sung as even eighth notes.

knew Ma - ry Lou __ we'd nev - er part, __ so hel - lo __

Chorus

Gtrs. 1, 2 & 3: w/ Rhy. Figs. 1, 1A & Riff A
2nd time, Gtrs. 1, 2 & 3: w/ Rhy. Figs. 1, 1A & Riff A (1st 15 meas.)

Ma - ry Lou, good-bye heart. Sweet Ma - ry Lou — I'm

so — in love — with you. — I knew Ma - ry Lou

we'd nev - er part, — so hel - lo — Ma - ry Lou, — good-bye — heart.

Guitar Solo

Gtrs. 1 & 3: w/ Rhy. Fig. 1 & Riff A

Gtr. 2

*w/ pick & fingers
*P.M. downstemmed notes throughout

**Bend string down.

⊕ Coda

Hey Joe

Words and Music by Billy Roberts

I said, where you go-in' with that gun in your hand? ___ Al - right.

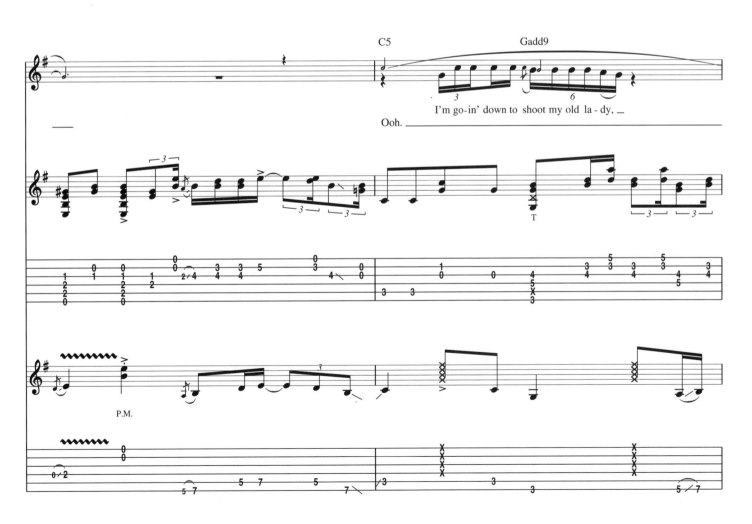

I'm go-in' down to shoot my old la - dy, ___

Ooh. ___

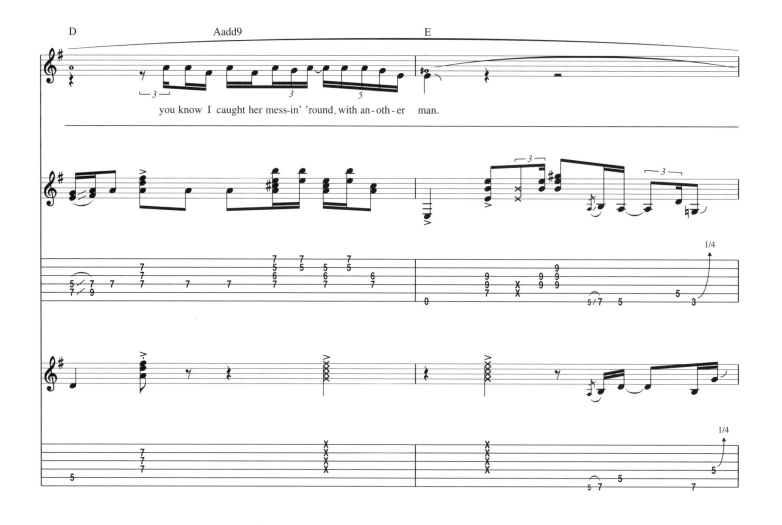

you know I caught her mess-in' 'round with an-oth-er man.

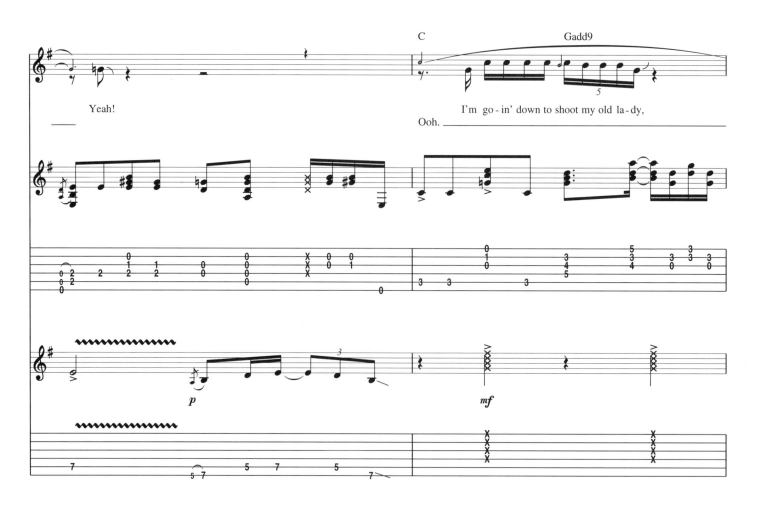

Yeah!

Ooh.

I'm go-in' down to shoot my old la-dy,

you know I caught her mess-in' 'round with an-oth-er man. _ Huh! And that ain't

too cool.
___)
(Ah. ___

Verse

2. Uh, hey, _ Joe, _ I heard you . shot your

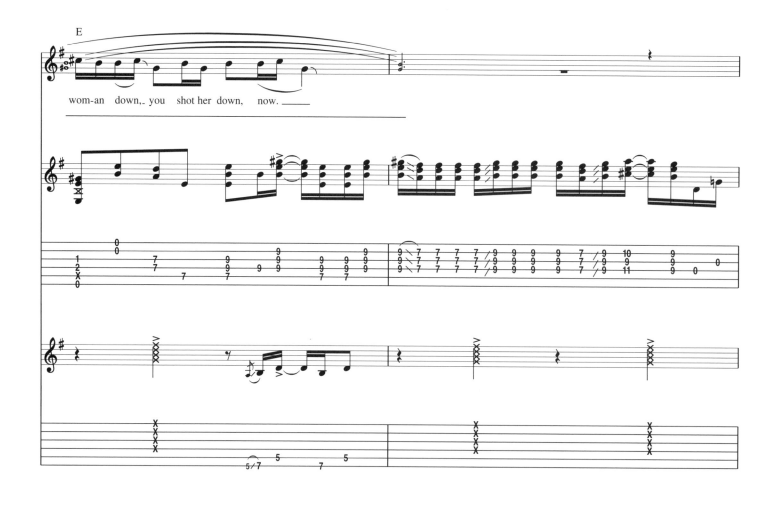

wom-an down,_ you shot her down, now. ____

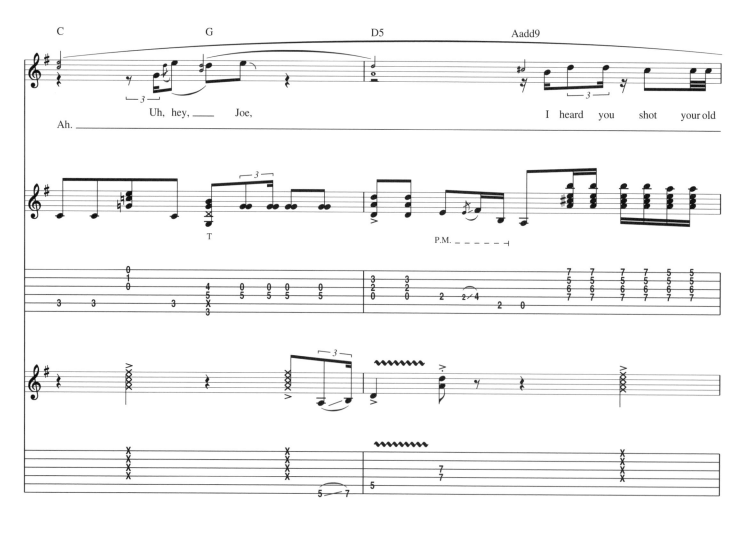

C   G   D5   Aadd9

Ah. ____   Uh, hey, ____ Joe,   I heard you shot your old

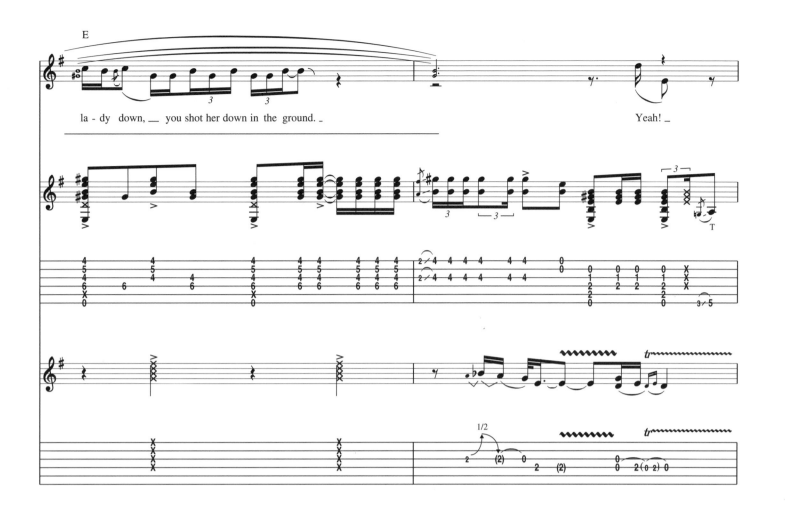

la - dy down, __ you shot her down in the ground. __   Yeah! __

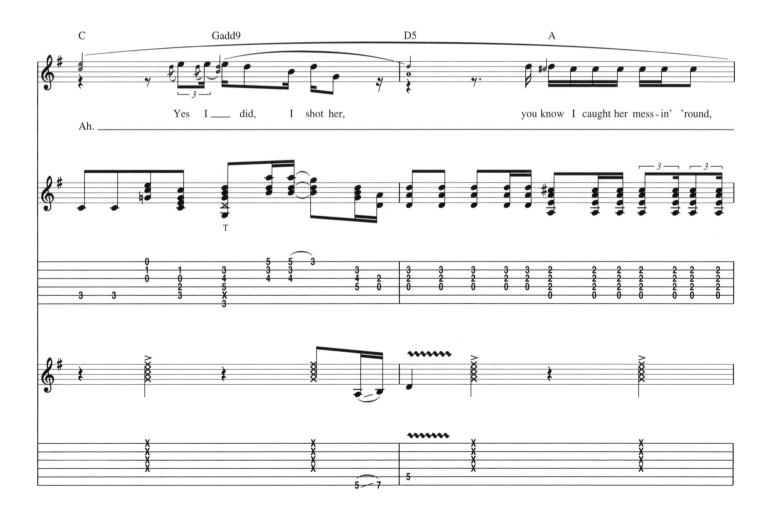

Ah. _____   Yes I __ did,   I shot her,   you know I caught her mess - in' 'round,

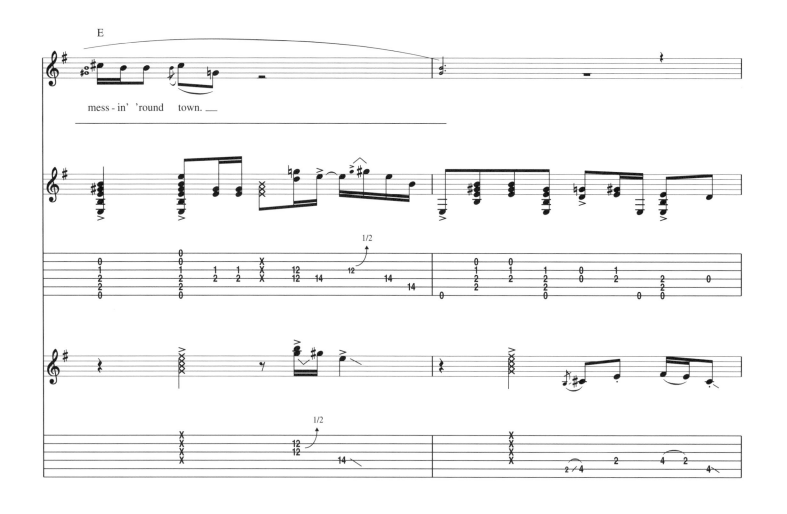

mess-in' 'round   town. __

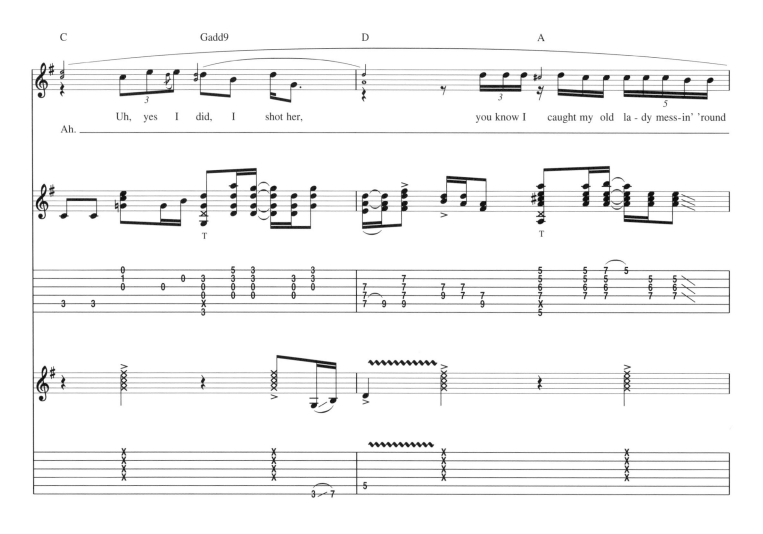

Uh, yes I did, I   shot her,   you know I   caught my old la - dy mess-in' 'round

Ah. __

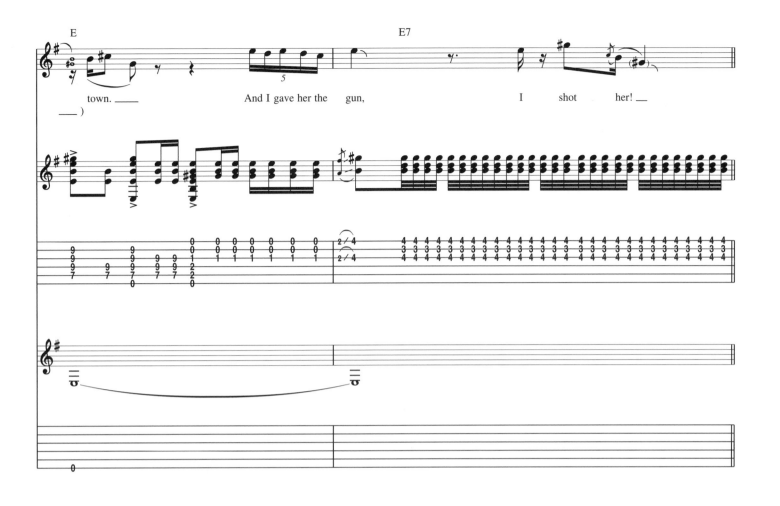

town. _____   And I gave her the   gun,   I   shot   her! __
_____)

Guitar Solo

(Woo! _____)   Ah! _____   Hey,   Joe! _____   Al - right!_

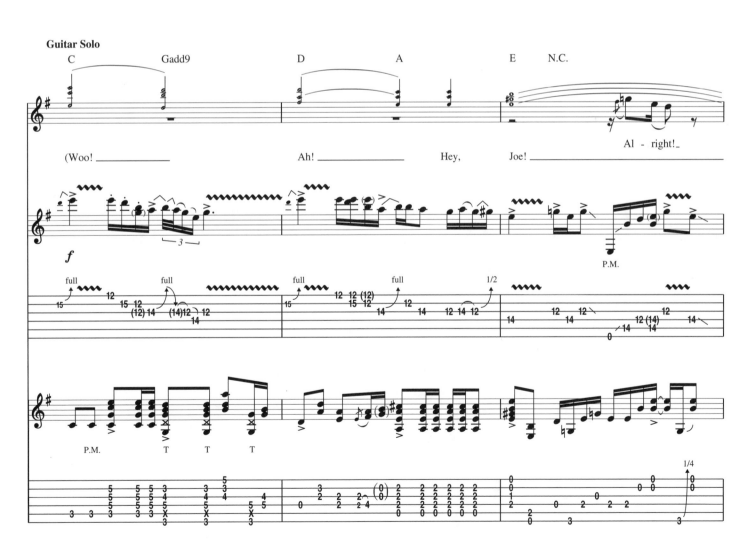

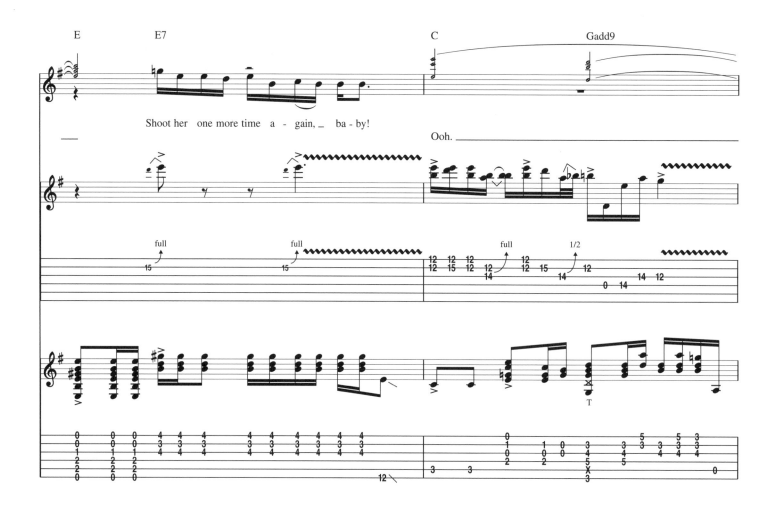

Shoot her one more time a - gain, __ ba - by!

Ooh. _____

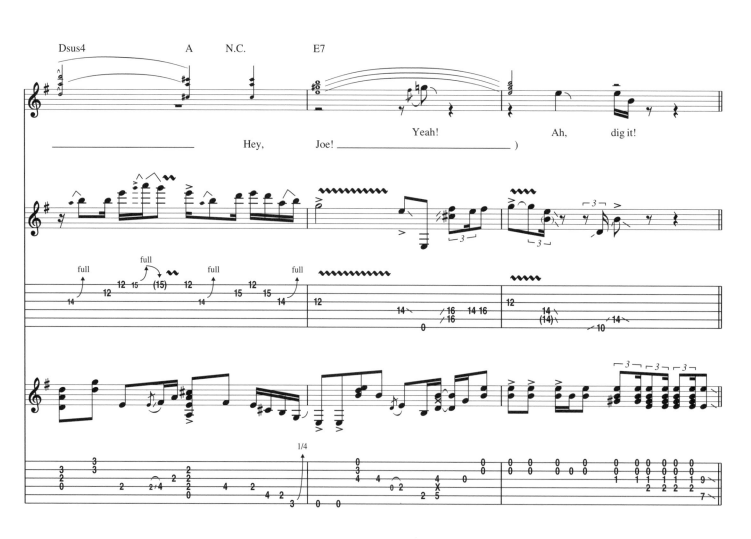

Hey, Joe! _____)

Yeah! _____ Ah, dig it!

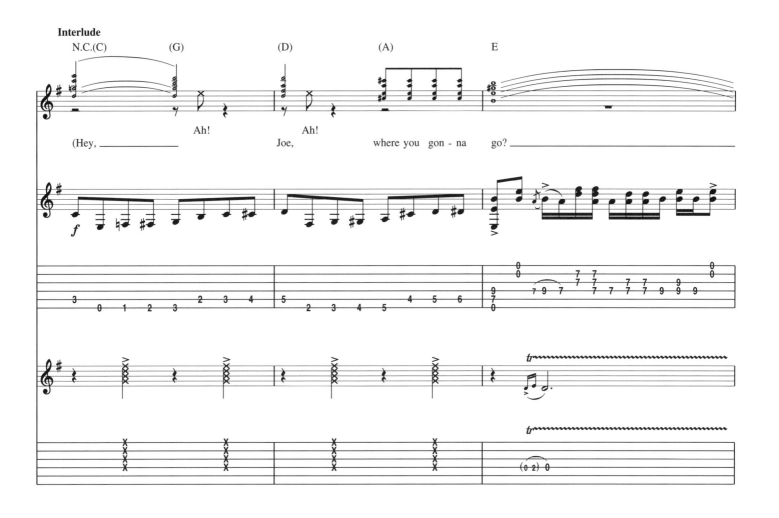

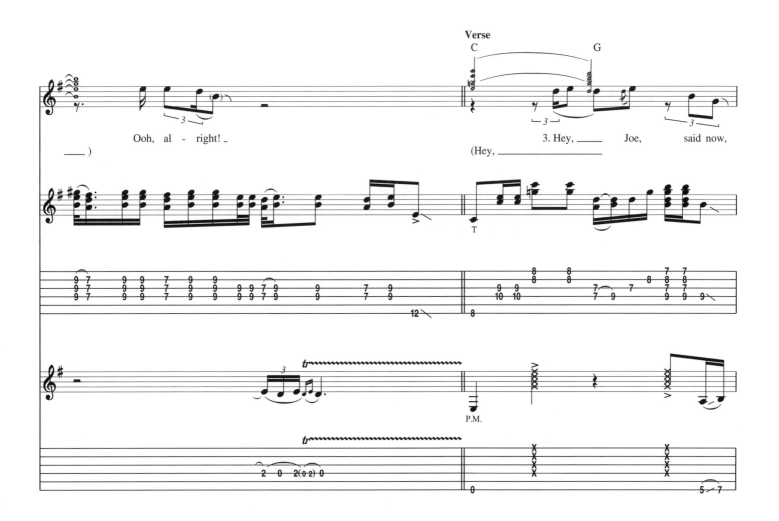

uh, where you gon-na run to now, __ where you gon-na run to? ___   Yeah.

Joe,   where   you   gon - na   go?_____

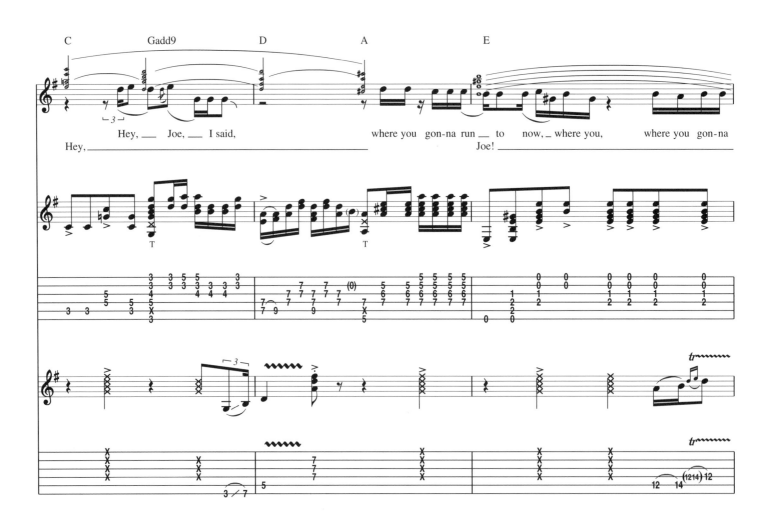

Hey, ___ Joe, ___ I said,   where you gon-na run __ to now, __ where you,   where you gon-na

Hey,_____   Joe! _____

go? — Well, dig it! I'm go-in' way down south, — way down — to
Hey,

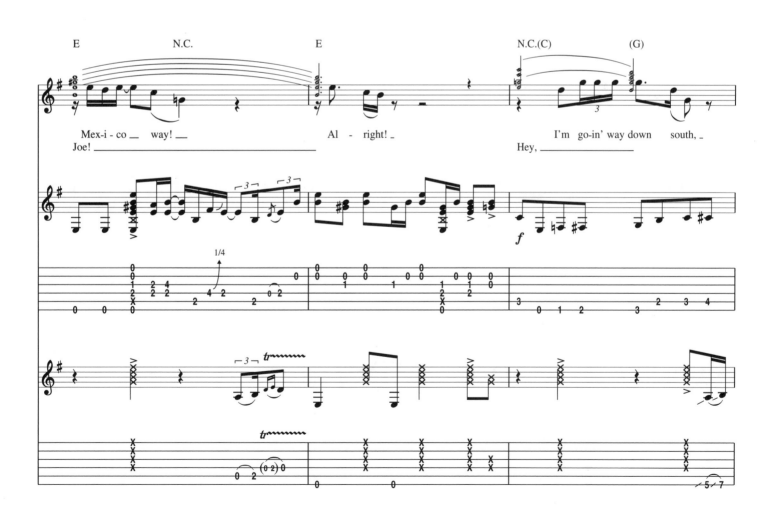

Mex-i-co — way! — Al - right! — I'm go-in' way down south, —
Joe! Hey,

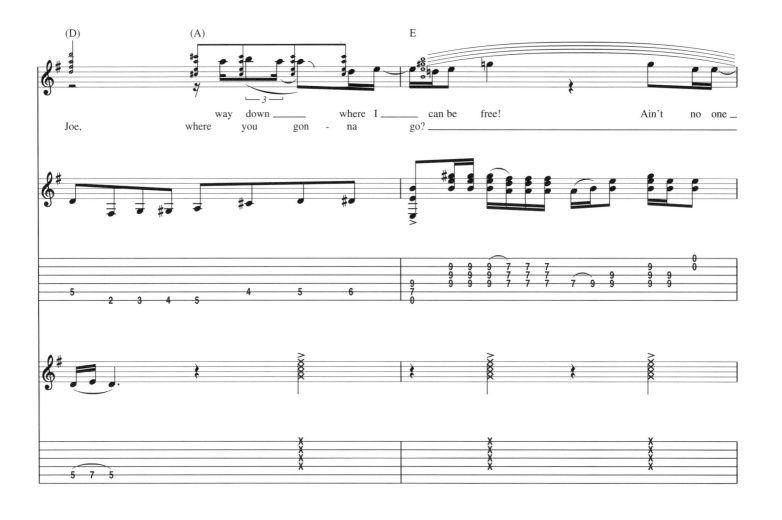

way down _____ where I _____ can be free! Aint no one _____
Joe, where you gon-na go? _____

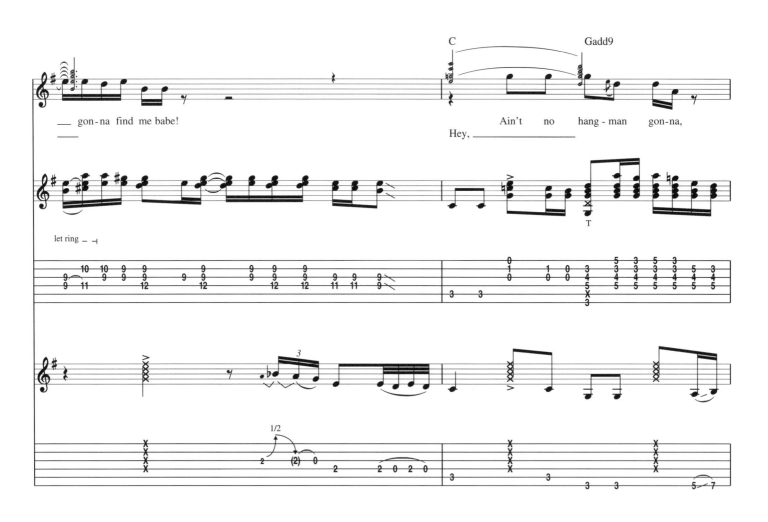

_____ gon-na find me babe!
_____ Hey, _____

Aint no hang-man gon-na,

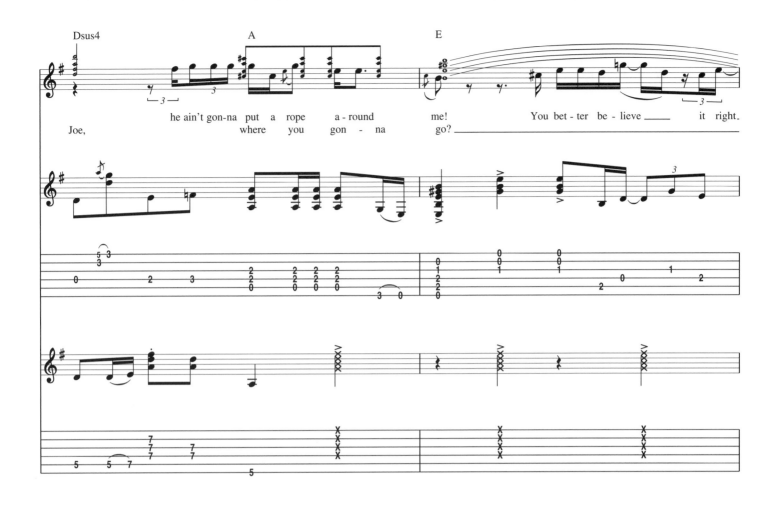

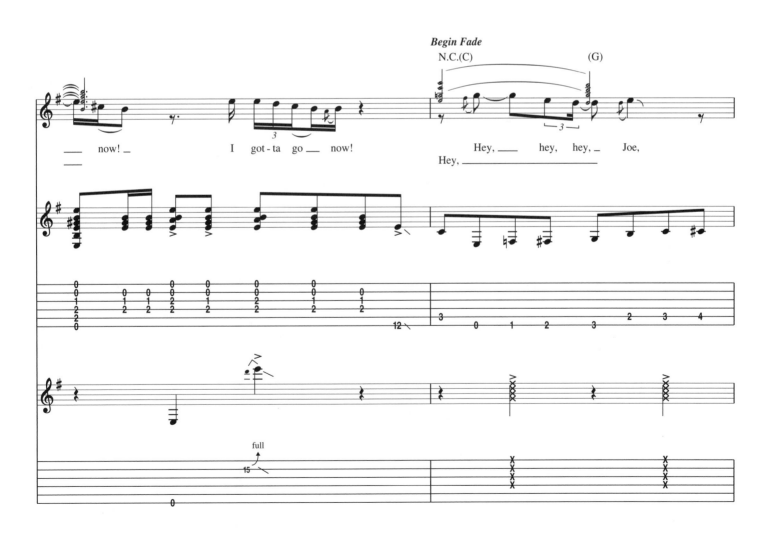

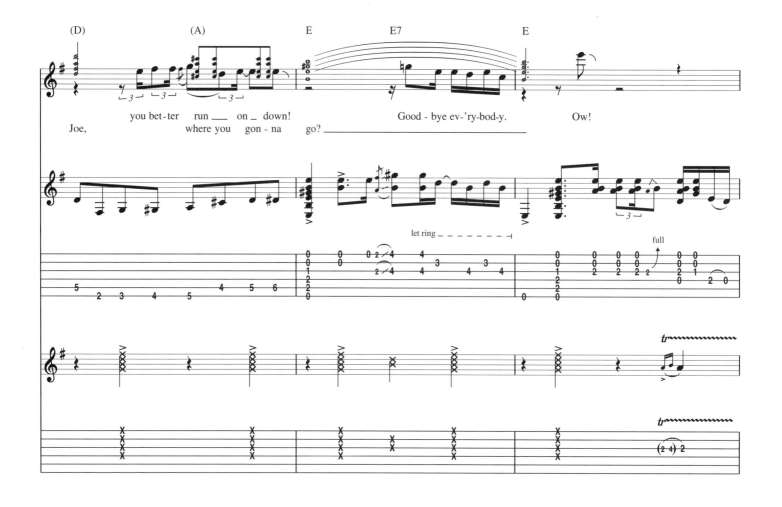

you bet-ter run ___ on _ down!   Good - bye ev-'ry-bod-y.   Ow!

Joe,   where you gon - na   go? _____

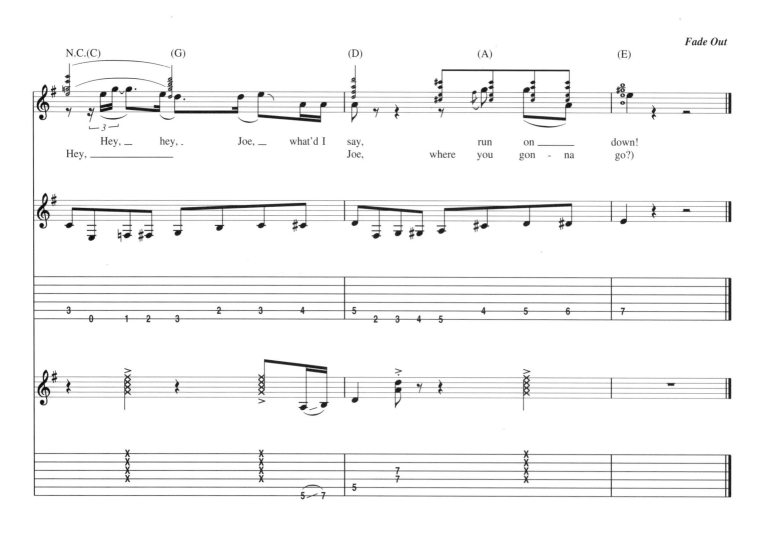

Hey, ___ hey, ___   Joe, ___ what'd I say,   run on _____ down!

Hey, _____   Joe,   where you gon - na   go?)

Hush

Words and Music by Joe South

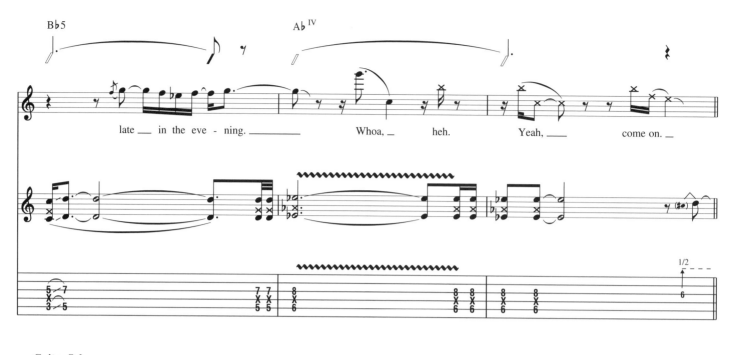

late __ in the eve - ning. _____ Whoa, __ heh. Yeah, ___ come on. __

Guitar Solo
Gtr. 1 tacet
*Fm7

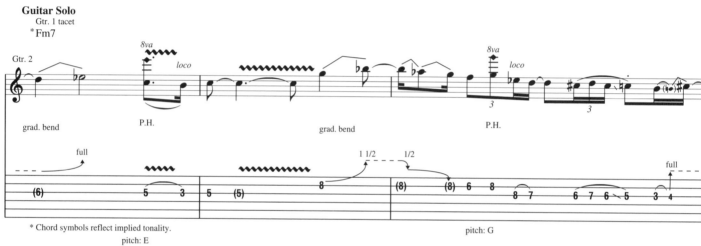

Gtr. 2

grad. bend

P.H.

grad. bend

P.H.

* Chord symbols reflect implied tonality.

pitch: E

pitch: G

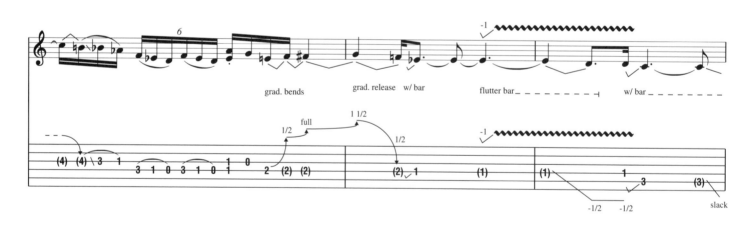

grad. bends

grad. release   w/ bar

flutter bar _ _ _ _ _

w/ bar _ _ _ _

slack

Harmonica Solo
G

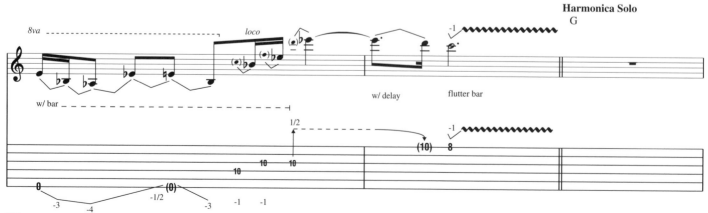

w/ bar _ _ _ _ _ _ _ _ _

w/ delay

flutter bar

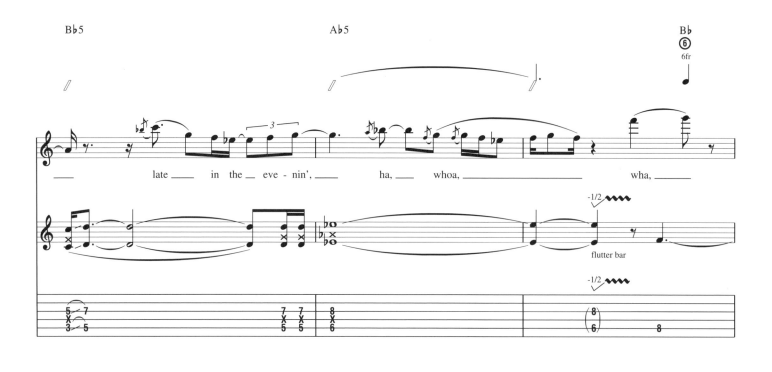

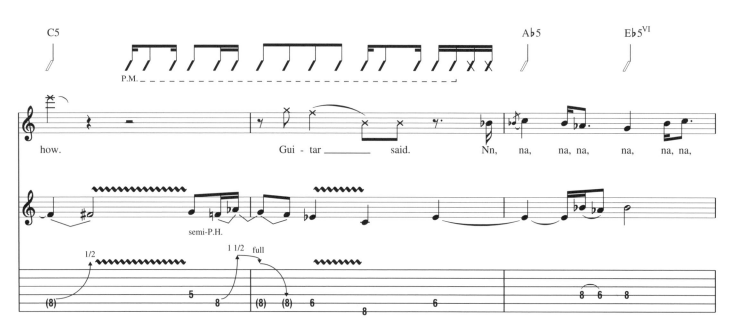

* Set one octave lower.

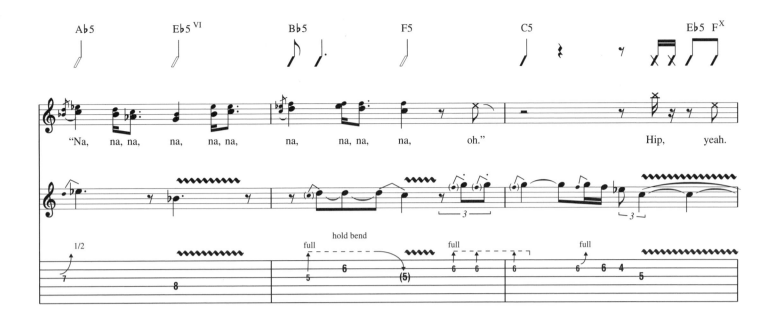

"Na, na, na, na, na, na, na, na, na, na, oh."   Hip,   yeah.

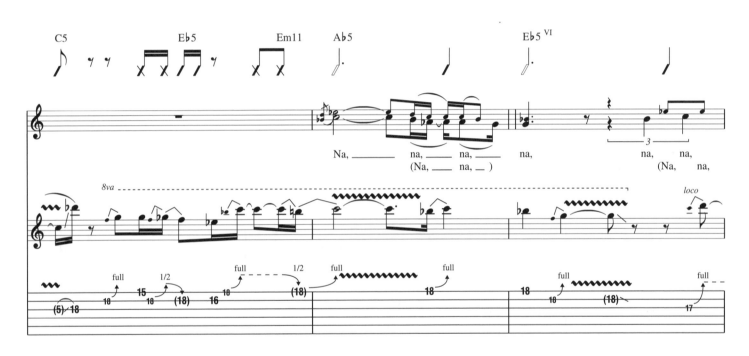

Na, _____ na, _____ na, _____ na,   na,   na,
(Na, _____ na, _____)
(Na,   na,

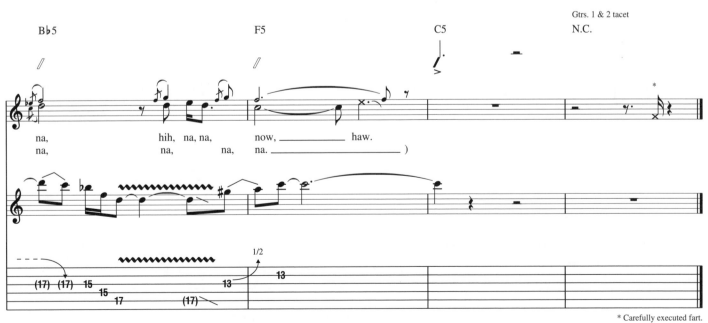

Gtrs. 1 & 2 tacet

na,   hih, na, na,   now, _____ haw.
na,   na,   na,   na. _____)

* Carefully executed fart.

I Can See for Miles

Words and Music by Peter Townshend

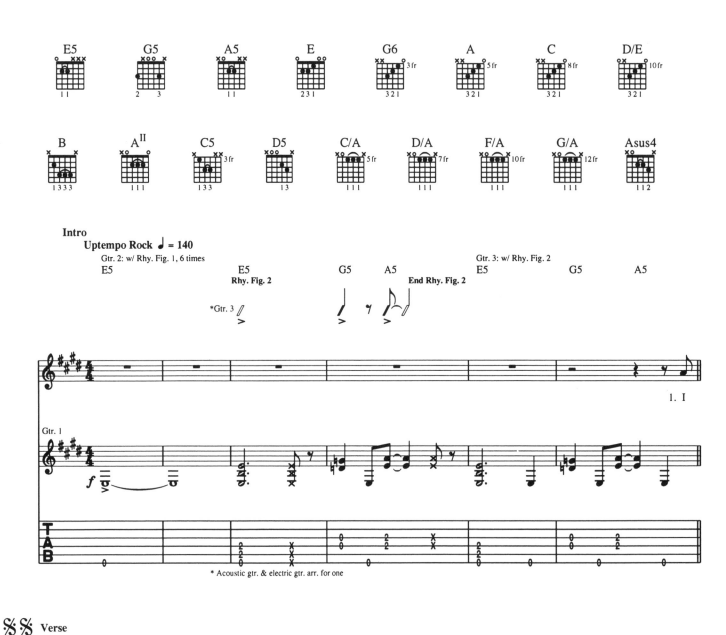

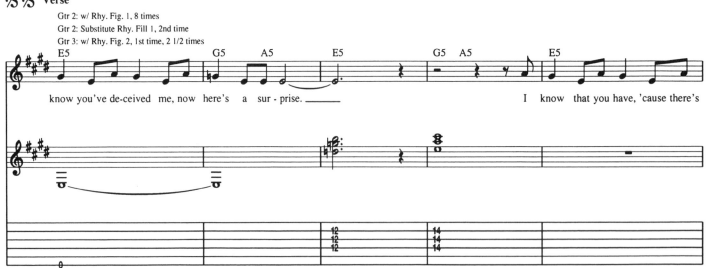

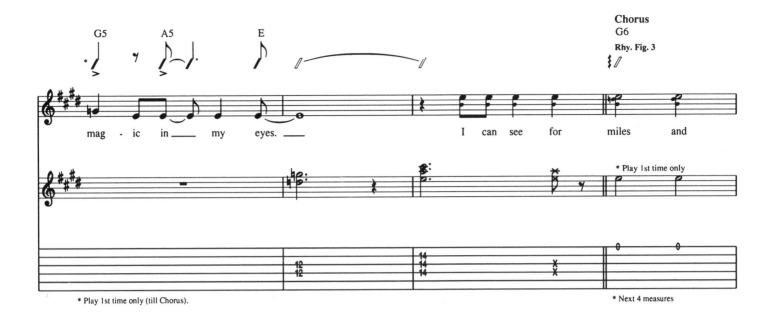

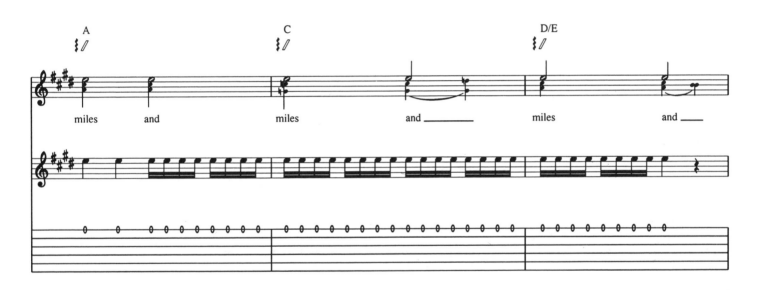

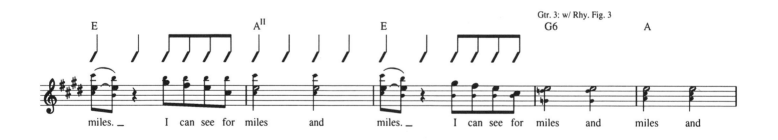

Verse

Gtr. 2: w/ Rhy. Fig. 1, 8 times
Gtr. 3: w/ Rhy. Fig. 2, 3 times

E5   G5   A5   E5   G5   A5

3. You took ad-van-tage of my trust in you when I was so far a-way.

E5   G5   A5   E5

I saw you hold-in' lots of oth-er guys, and now you've got the nerve to say ___ that you

Gtr. 1 out

Pre-Chorus

D.S. al Coda 1

A5   B   A5   B

Gtrs. 2 & 3

still want me. ___ Well, that's as may be, but you got-ta stand trial be-cause all the while, _____ I can see for

✠ *Coda 1*

Guitar Solo

Gtr. 2: w/ Rhy. Fig. 1, 10 times
Gtr. 3: w/ Rhy. Fig. 2, 3 times

Gtr. 1

E5   G5   A5   E5   G5   A5   E5   G5   A5

trem. pick -

D.S.S. al Coda 2

E5

4. I

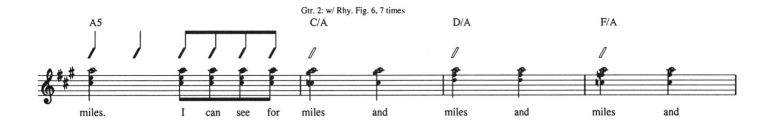

miles. I can see for miles and miles and miles and

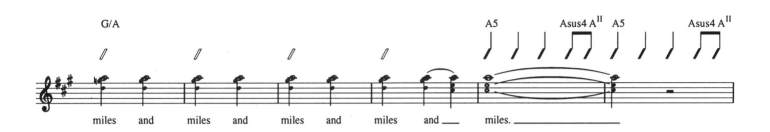

miles and miles and miles and miles and ___ miles. _____

Repeat and Fade

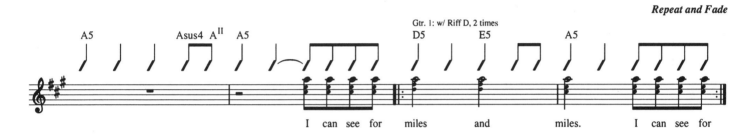

I can see for miles and miles. I can see for

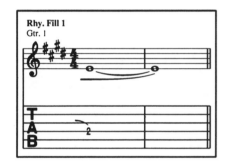

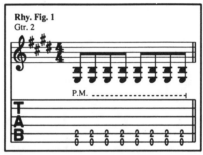

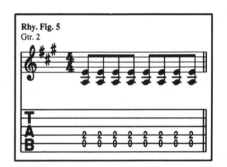

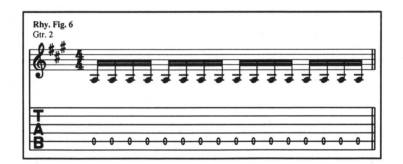

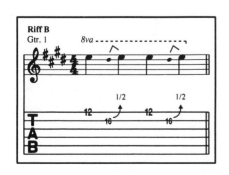

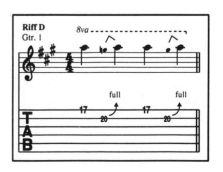

I Feel Fine

Words and Music by John Lennon and Paul McCartney

I Get Around

Words and Music by Brian Wilson and Mike Love

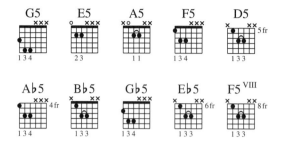

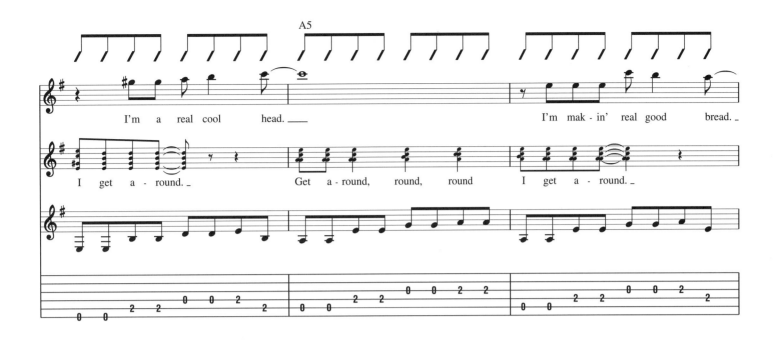

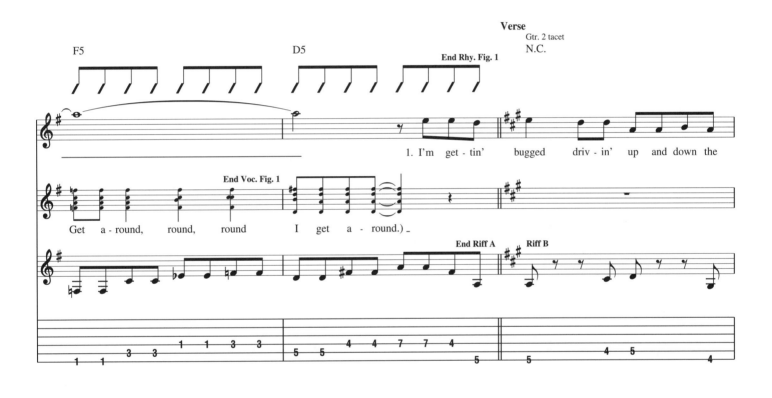

Gtr. 1: w/ Riff B

My bud-dies and me ___ are get-tin'

real well known. ___ Yeah, the bad guys know us and they leave us a-lone. I get a-

Chorus
Bkgd. Voc.: w/ Voc. Fig. 1
Gtr. 1: w/ Rhy. Riff A
Gtr. 2: w/ Rhy. Fig. 1

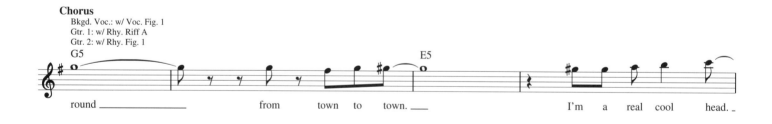

G5   E5

round _____   from town to town. ___   I'm a real cool head. _

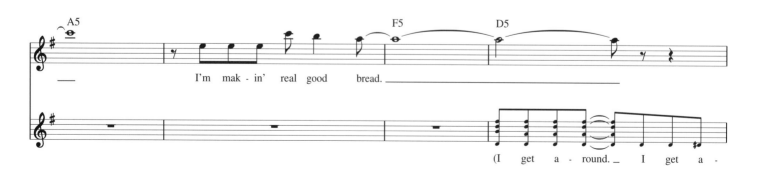

A5   F5   D5

___   I'm mak-in' real good bread. _____

(I get a-round. ___ I get a-

Guitar Solo

Get a - round, round, round.

round.) _____

(Round.) _____

(Oo, _____

*Chord symbols reflect overall harmony.

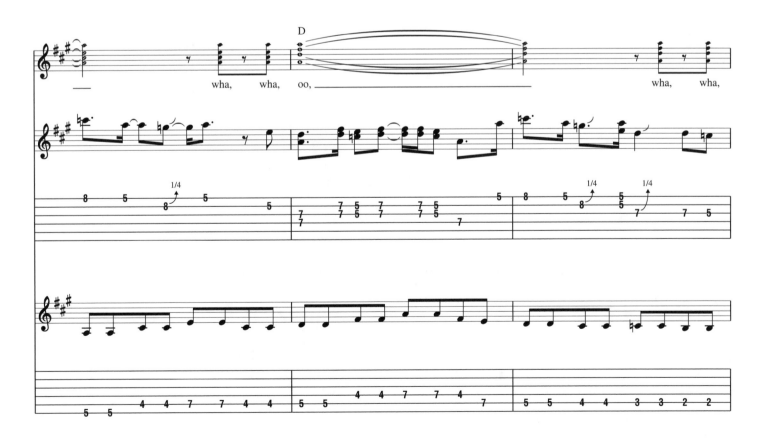

wha, wha, oo, _____ wha, wha,

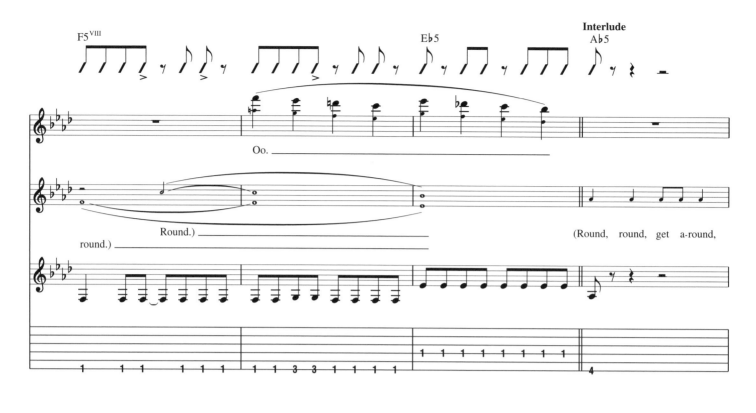

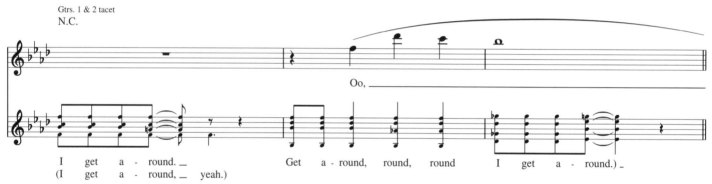

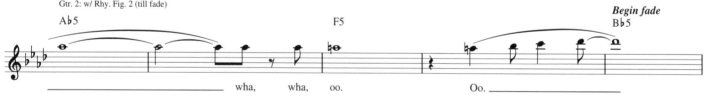

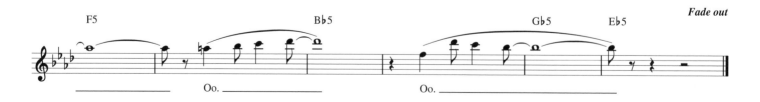

In the Midnight Hour

Words and Music by Steve Cropper and Wilson Pickett

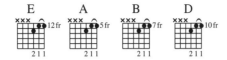

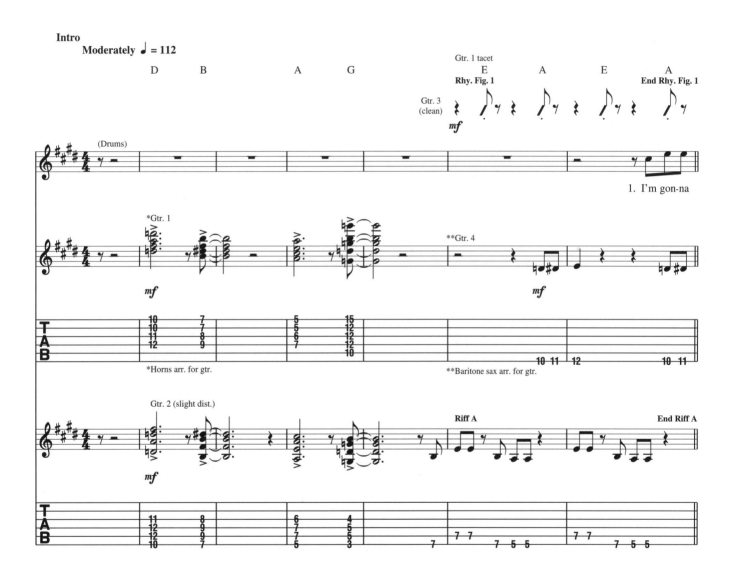

Verse

Gtrs. 2 & 3: w/ Riff A & Rhy. Fig. 1 (4 times)
2nd time, Gtr. 1 w/ Riff B
2nd time, Gtr. 4 tacet

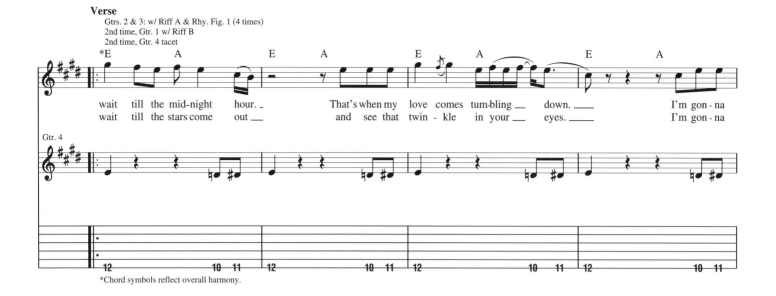

wait till the mid-night hour. _____ That's when my love comes tum-bling ___ down. ____ I'm gon - na
wait till the stars come out ___ and see that twin - kle in your ___ eyes. ____ I'm gon - na

Gtr. 4

*Chord symbols reflect overall harmony.

wait till the mid-night hour, ____ when there's no one else ___ a - round. _____ I'm gon - na
wait till the mid-night hour. ____ That's when my love be - gins _ to shine. _____ You're the

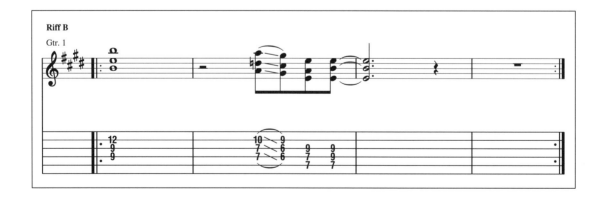

Riff B

Gtr. 1

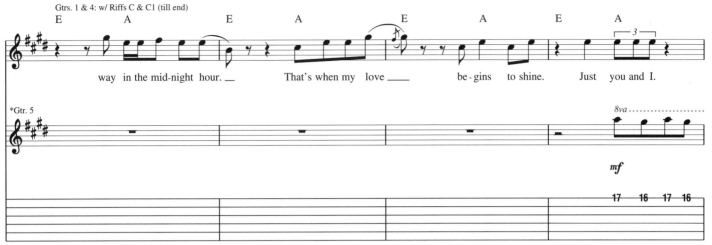

*Trumpet arr. for gtr.

*Trumpet arr. for gtr.

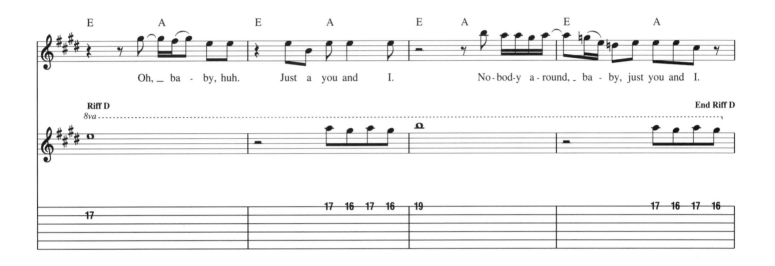

Jingo (Jin-Go-Lo-Ba)

By Michael Olatunji

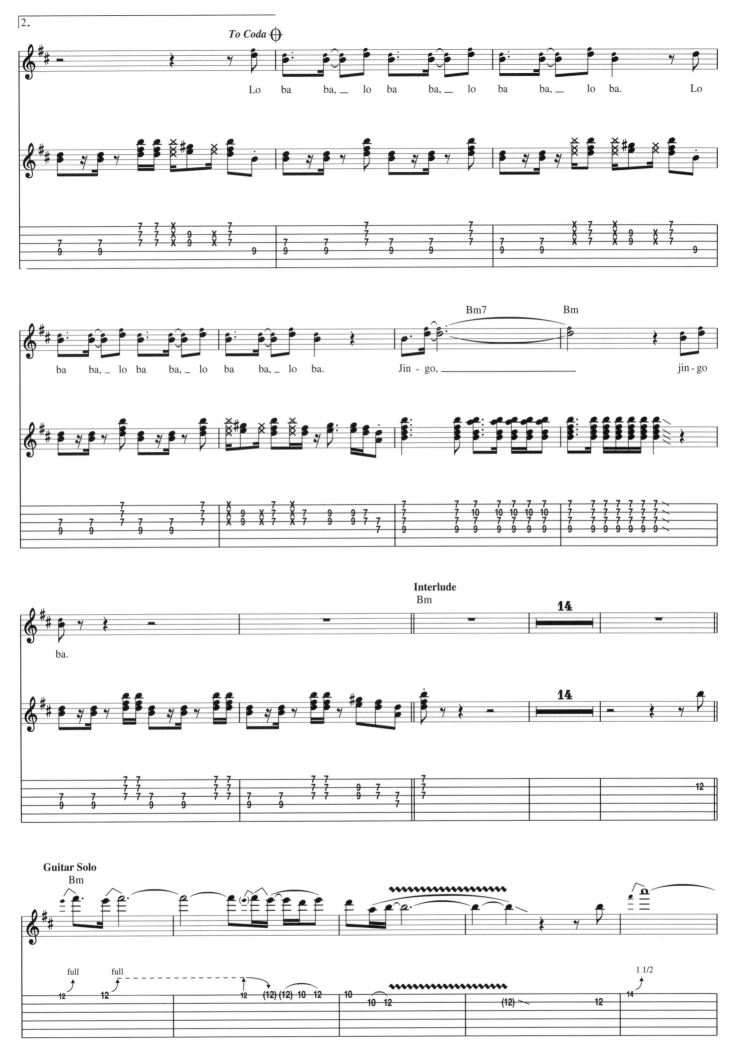

Let's Live for Today

Words and Music by Guido Cenciarelli, Giulio Rapetti and Norman David

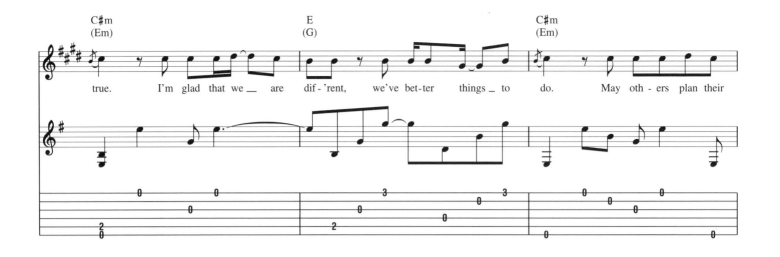

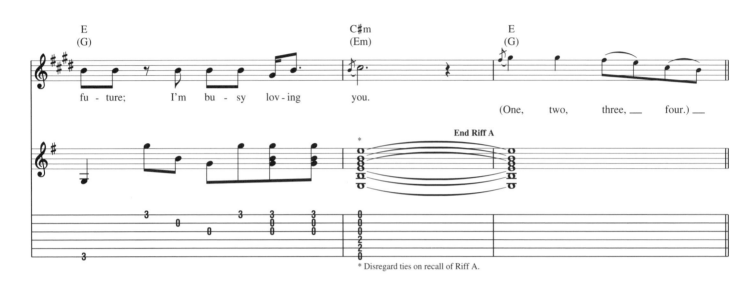

*Disregard ties on recall of Riff A.

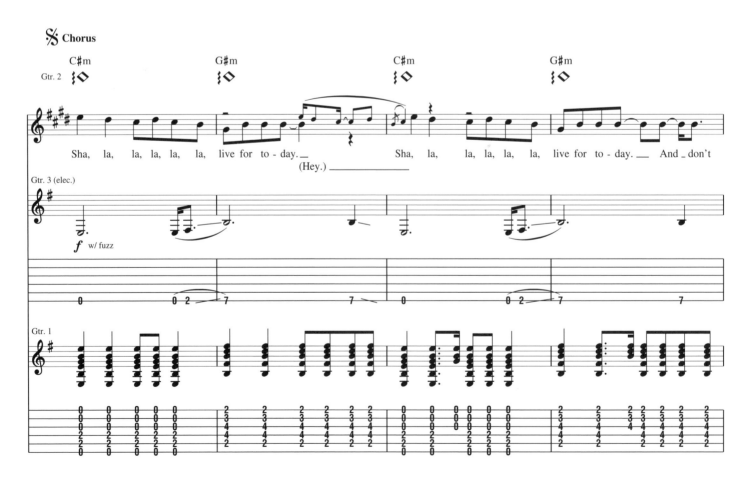

⊕ Coda 1

Interlude

Louie, Louie

Words and Music by Richard Berry

* Lyrics omitted at the request of the publisher.

Gtr. 1: w/Rhy. Fig. 2, 1st 2 meas.

My Girl

Words and Music by William "Smokey" Robinson and Ronald White

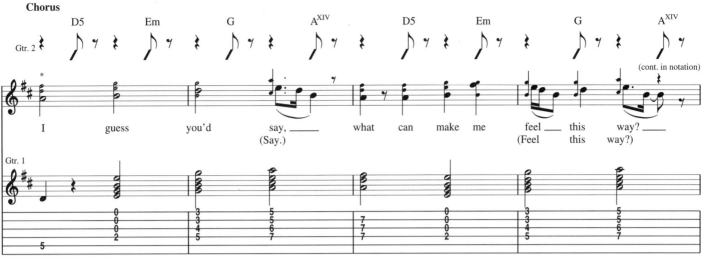

*Bkgd. Voc. low in mix

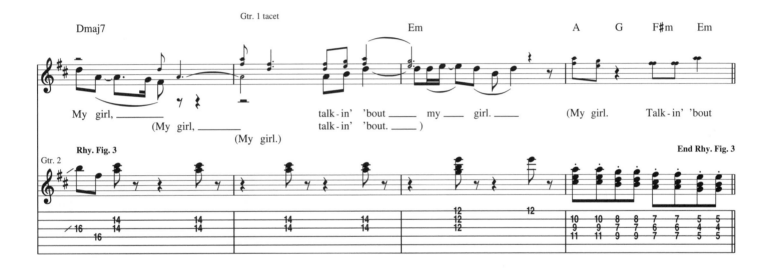

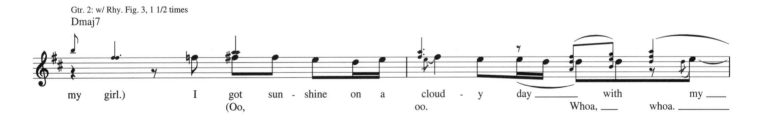

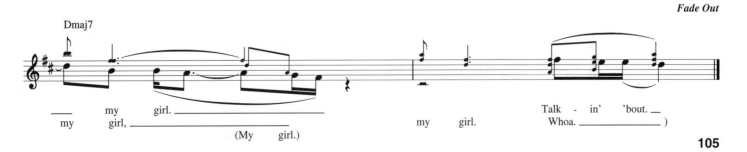

Oh, Pretty Woman

Words and Music by Roy Orbison and Bill Dees

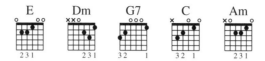

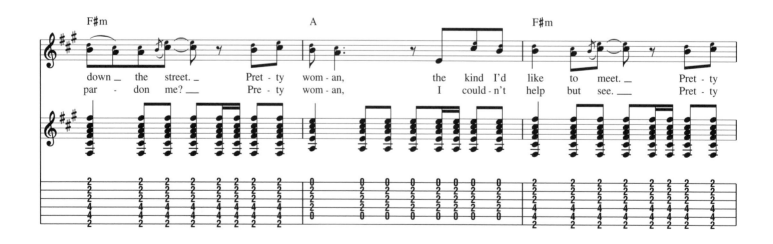

On the Road Again

Words and Music by Alan Wilson and Floyd Jones

Intro

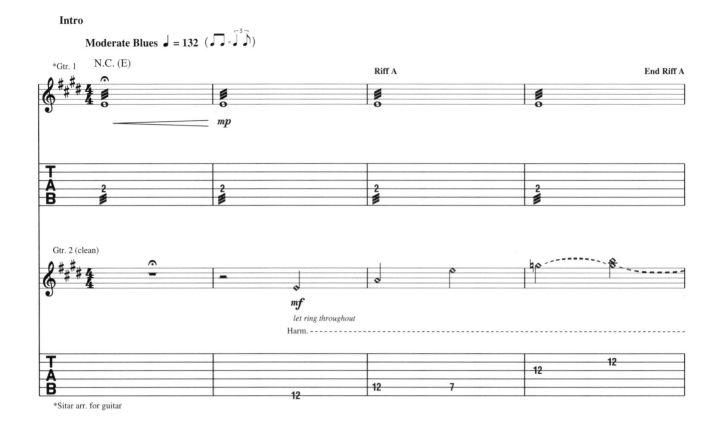

*Sitar arr. for guitar

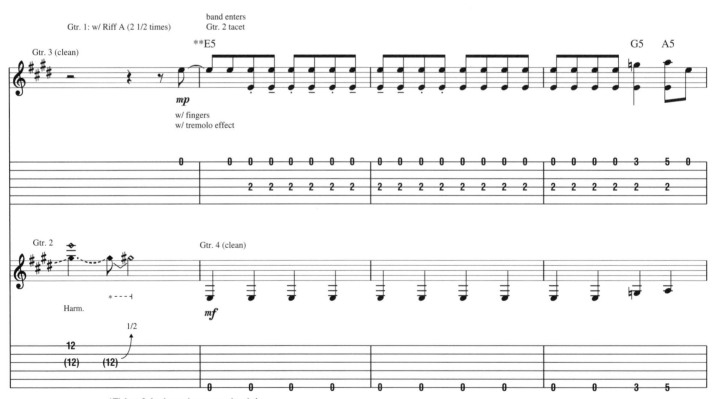

*Tighten 3rd string tuning peg to raise pitch.

**Chord symbols reflect basic harmony.

⊕ Coda

Outro - Harmonica Solo

Gtr. 1 w/ Riff A (12 times)
Gtrs. 3 & 4: w/ Riffs B & B1 (4 1/2 times)

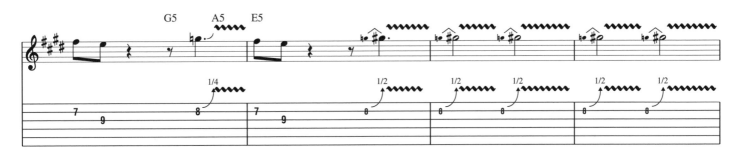

Begin fade

*Except Gtr. 1

Fade out   *Free time*

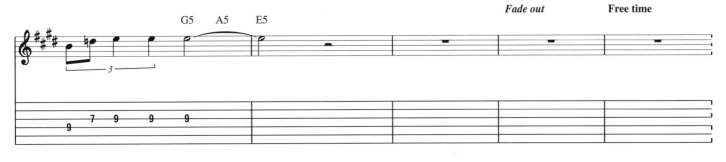

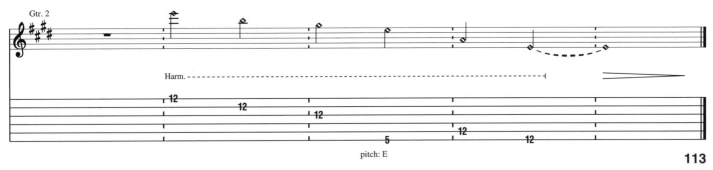

pitch: E

The Promised Land

Words and Music by Chuck Berry

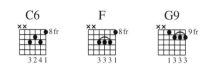

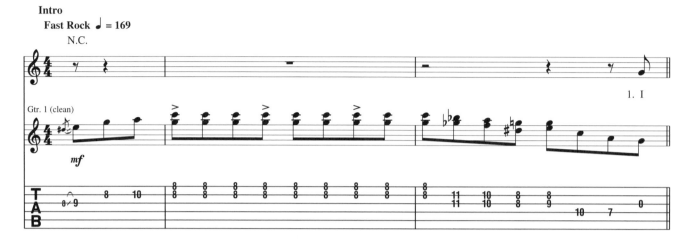

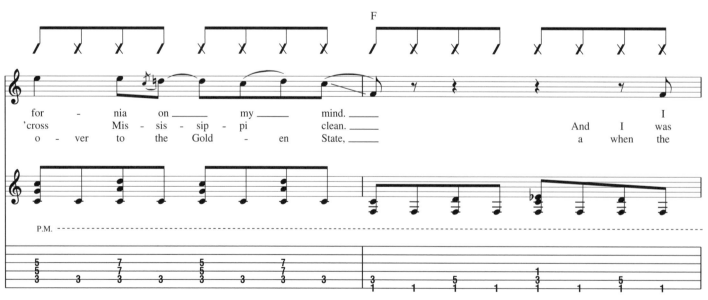

strad - dled that Grey - hound and rode ___ him in - to Ral - eigh and on ___
on that Mid - night Fly - er out of Bir - ming - ham,
pi - lot told ___ us in thir - teen min - utes he would

___ a - cross Car - o - line. ___ We
smok - in' in - to New Or - leans. ___
set us at the ter - mi - nal gate. ___

End Rhy. Fig. 1A

End Rhy. Fig. 1

Gtr. 1: w/ Rhy. Fig. 1 (1 3/4 times)
Gtr. 2: w/ Rhy. Fig. 1A (2 times)

stopped in Char - lotte, we by - passed Rock - hill, we nev - er was a min - ute ___ late. ___
Some - bod - y help ___ me get out ___ of Lou - 'si - an - a, just help me get to Hous - ton town. ___
Swing low char - i - ot, come ___ down eas - y, tax - i to the ter - mi - nal zone. ___

___ A we was nine - ty miles out of At - lan - ta by sun - down, roll -
There are a peo - ple there ___ who care ___ a lit - tle 'bout me and they
Cut your en - gines and cool ___ your wings ___ and let me

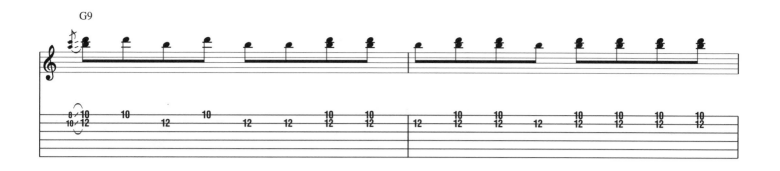

D.S. al Coda 1

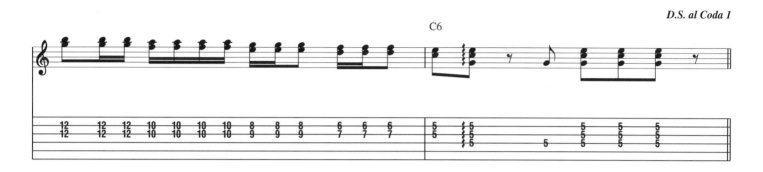

⊕ Coda 1

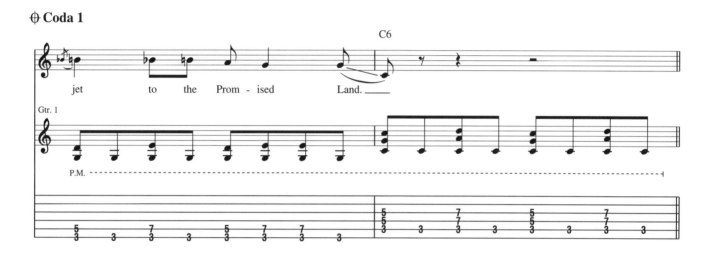

jet   to   the   Prom - ised   Land. ____

Guitar Solo

Gtr. 2: w/ Rhy. Fig. 1A

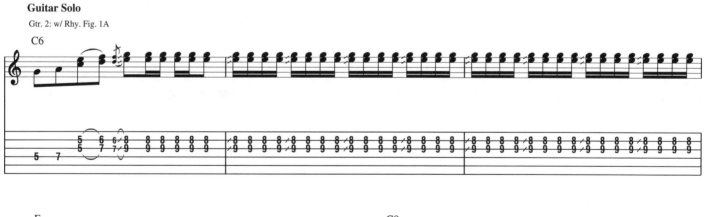

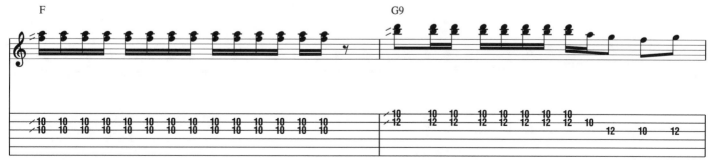

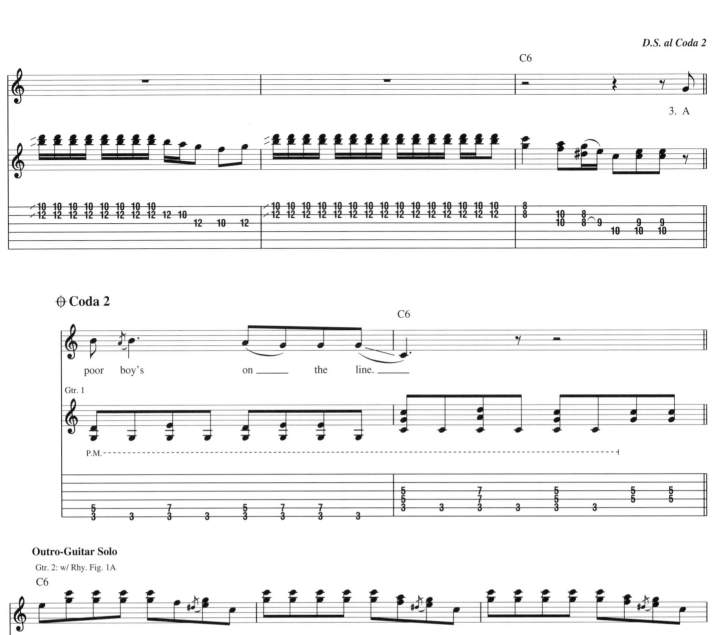

⊕ Coda 2

poor   boy's   on _____   the   line. _____

Outro-Guitar Solo

Gtr. 2: w/ Rhy. Fig. 1A

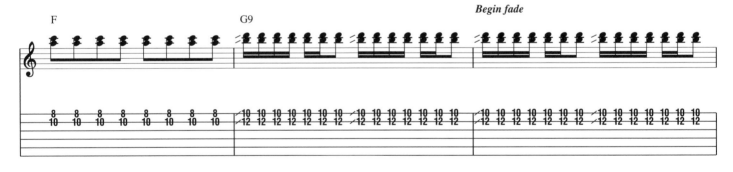

Begin fade

Fade out

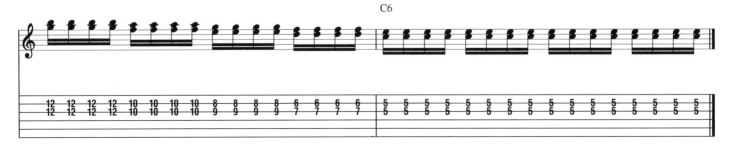

Somebody to Love

Words and Music by Darby Slick

Verse

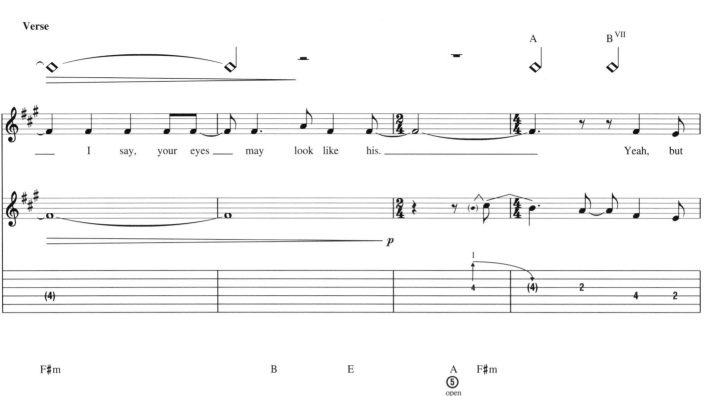

I say, your eyes ___ may look like his. _____ Yeah, but

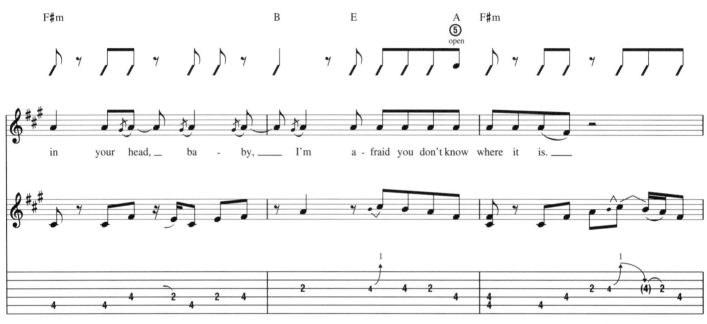

in your head, ___ ba — by, ___ I'm a-fraid you don't know where it is. ___

Chorus

Gtr. 1: w/ Rhy. Fig. 1

Don't you ___ want some-bod-y to love? ___ Don't ___ you
(Don't you

Outro-Guitar Solo

Soul Man

Words and Music by Isaac Hayes and David Porter

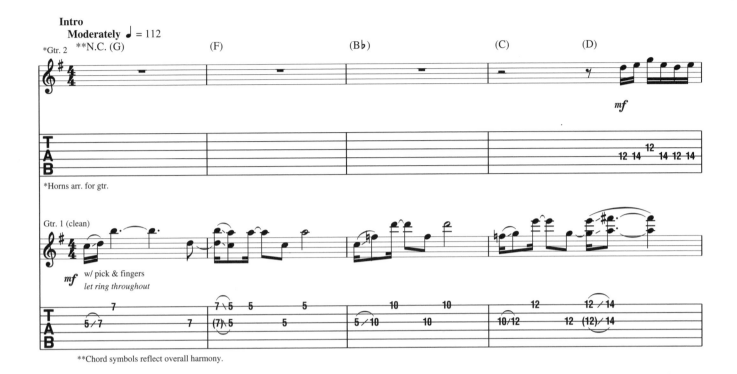

*Horns arr. for gtr.

**Chord symbols reflect overall harmony.

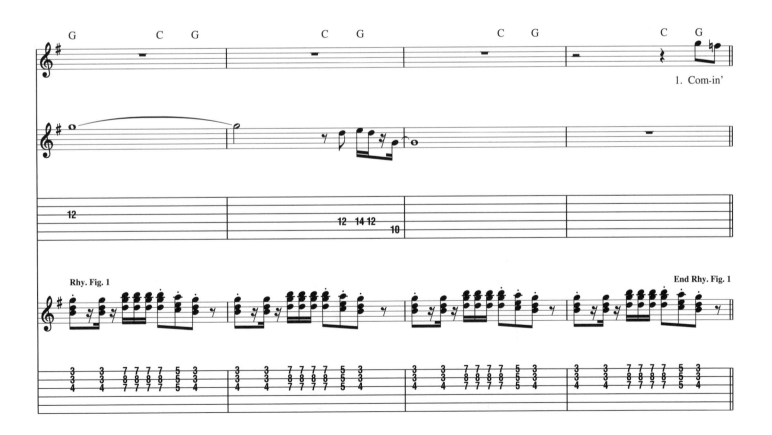

Gtr. 1: w/ Rhy. Fig. 1 (2 times)
2nd & 3rd times, Gtr. 2: w/ Riff C

Gtr. 2: w/ Riff A (3 times)

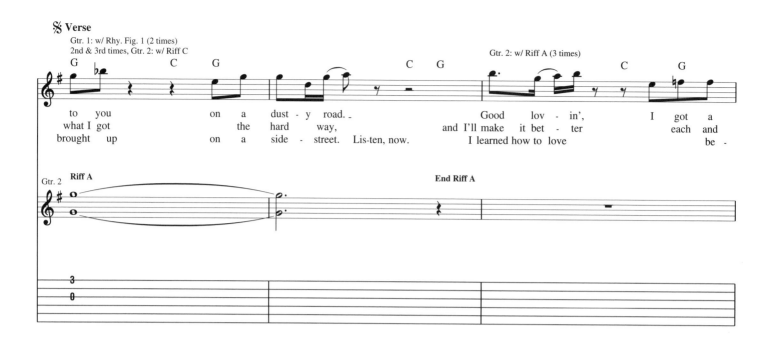

to you　on a　dust-y road. ＿　Good lov-in',　I got a
what I got　the hard　way,　and I'll make it bet-ter　each and
brought up　on a　side-street. Lis-ten, now.　I learned how to love　be-

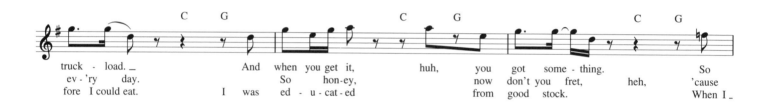

truck-load. ＿　And when you get it,　huh,　you got some-thing.　So
ev-'ry day.　So hon-ey,　now don't you fret, heh,　'cause
fore I could eat.　I was ed-u-cat-ed　from good stock.　When I ＿

2nd time, To Coda 1 ⊕
3rd time, To Coda 2 ⊕

don't ＿ wor-ry,　'cause I'm com-in'.　I'm a
you ain't seen ＿　noth-ing yet.　
＿ start lov-in',　oh, I can't　stop.　

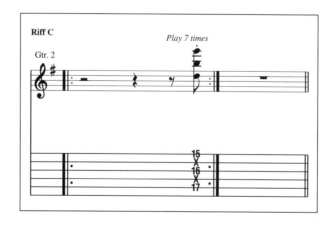

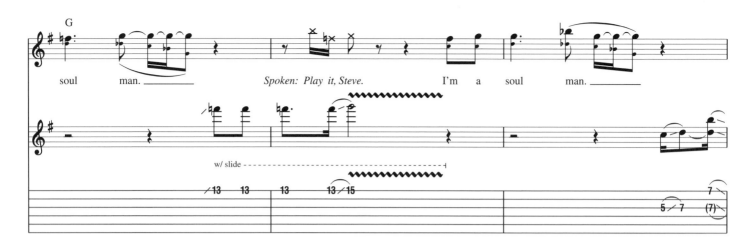

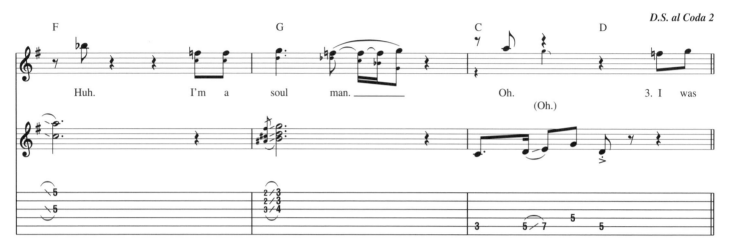

⊕ Coda 2
Chorus

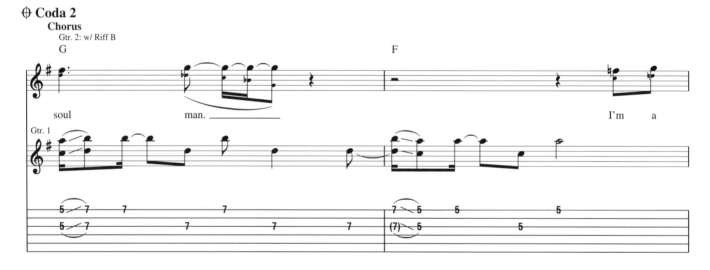

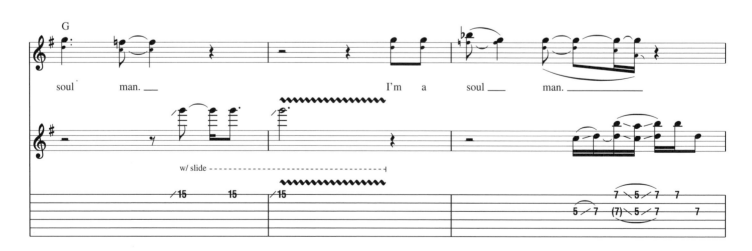

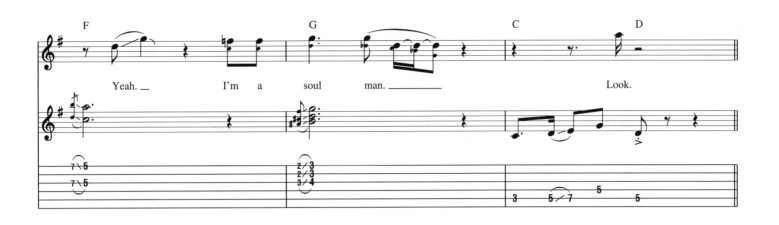

Yeah. ___ I'm a soul man. _____ Look.

Bridge

Grab a rope ___ and I'll pull you in. ___ Give you hope, and

Interlude

Gtr. 2 tacet

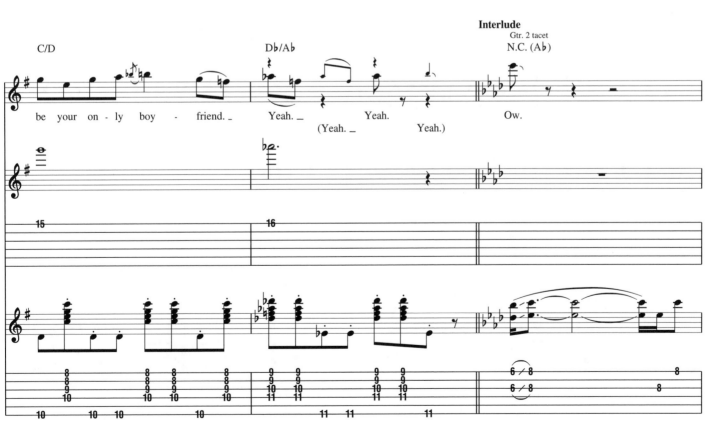

be your on-ly boy - friend. ___ Yeah. ___ Yeah. Ow.
(Yeah. ___ Yeah.)

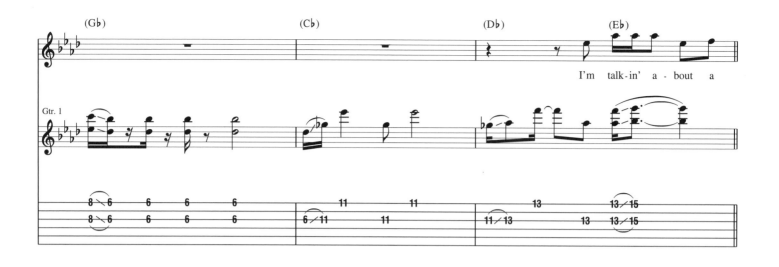

Suite: Judy Blue Eyes

Words and Music by Stephen Stills

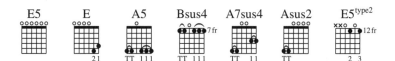

Gtrs. 1, 2 & 4: Open E5 tuning:
(low to high) E–E♭–E–E–B–E

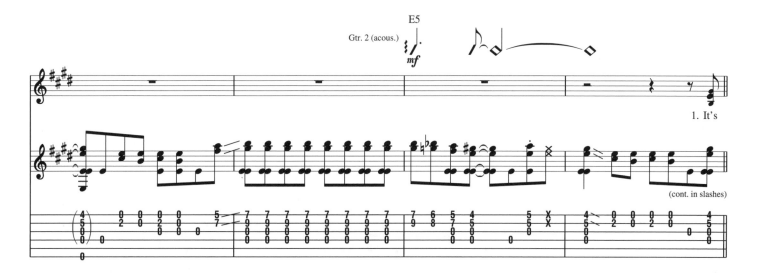

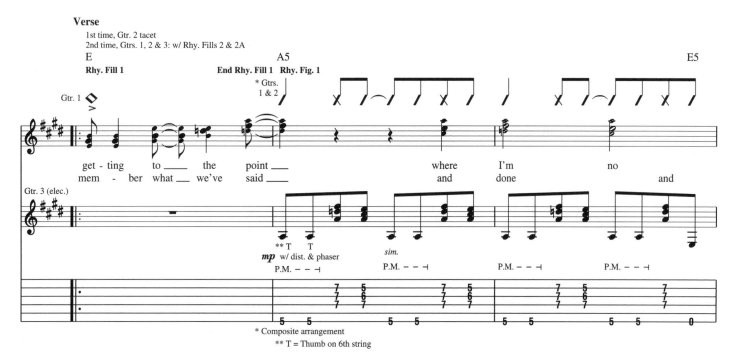

* Composite arrangement

** T = Thumb on 6th string

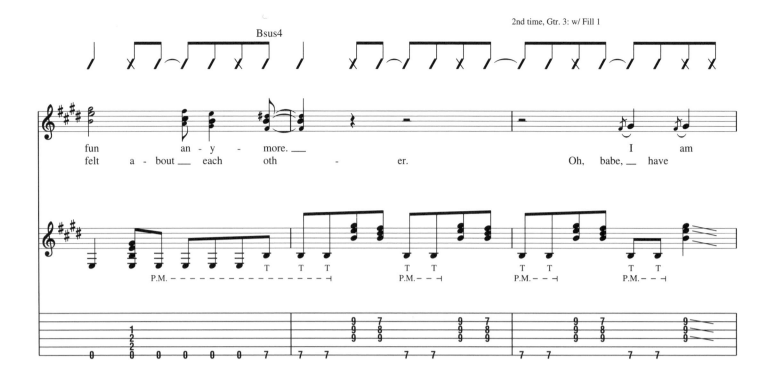

fun   an - y -   more.   I   am
felt   a - bout   each   oth   -   er.   Oh, babe,   have

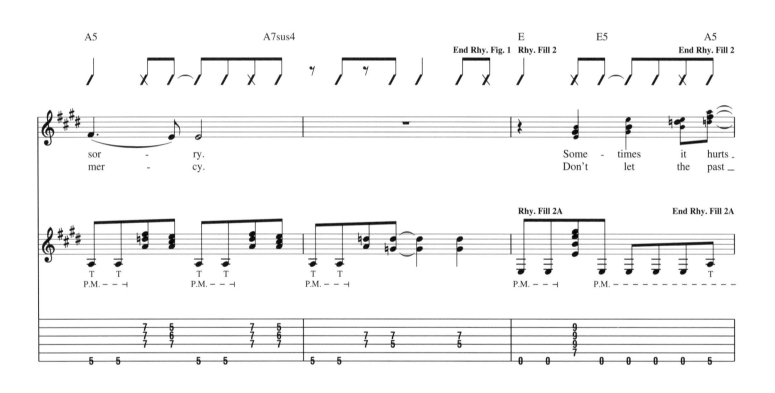

sor   -   ry.   Some   -   times   it   hurts
mer   -   cy.   Don't   let   the   past

134

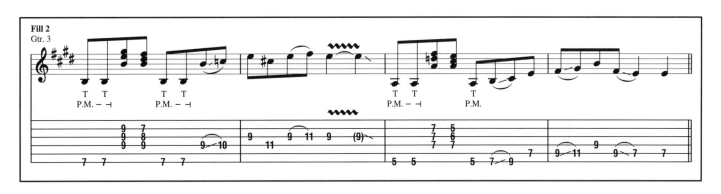

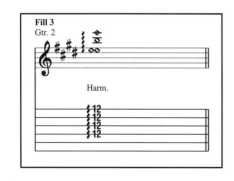

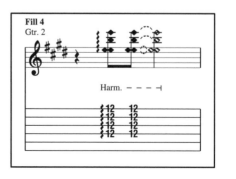

Bridge

Gtrs. 1 & 4: w/ Riffs A & A1 (1 1/2 times)
Gtr. 2 tacet

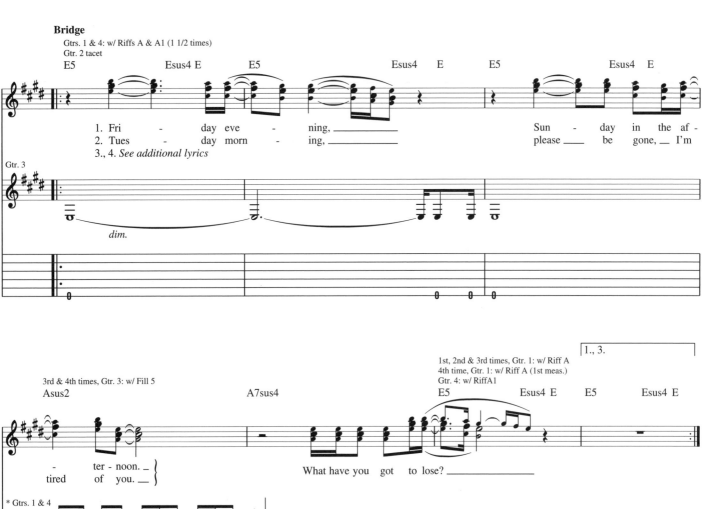

1. Fri - day eve - ning, _____
2. Tues - day morn - ing, _____
3., 4. *See additional lyrics*

Sun - day in the af -
please ___ be gone, ___ I'm

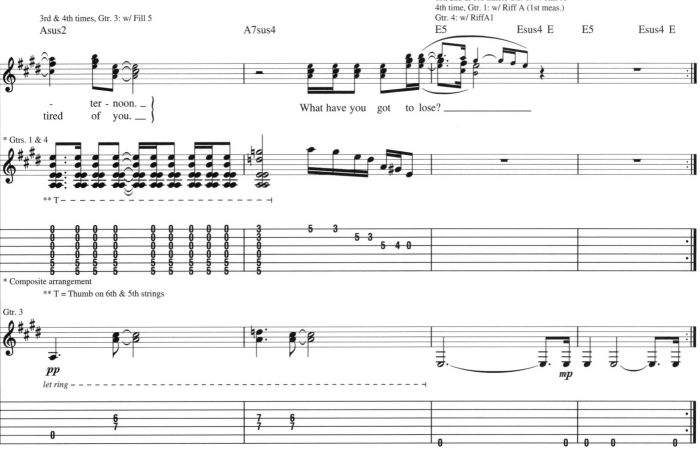

3rd & 4th times, Gtr. 3: w/ Fill 5

1st, 2nd & 3rd times, Gtr. 1: w/ Riff A
4th time, Gtr. 1: w/ Riff A (1st meas.)
Gtr. 4: w/ RiffA1

- ter - noon. ___
tired of you. ___

What have you got to lose? _____

* Gtrs. 1 & 4

** T

* Composite arrangement
   ** T = Thumb on 6th & 5th strings

Gtr. 3

pp
let ring
mp

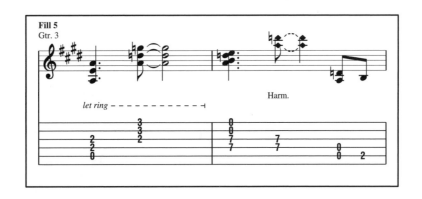

Fill 5
Gtr. 3

let ring
Harm.

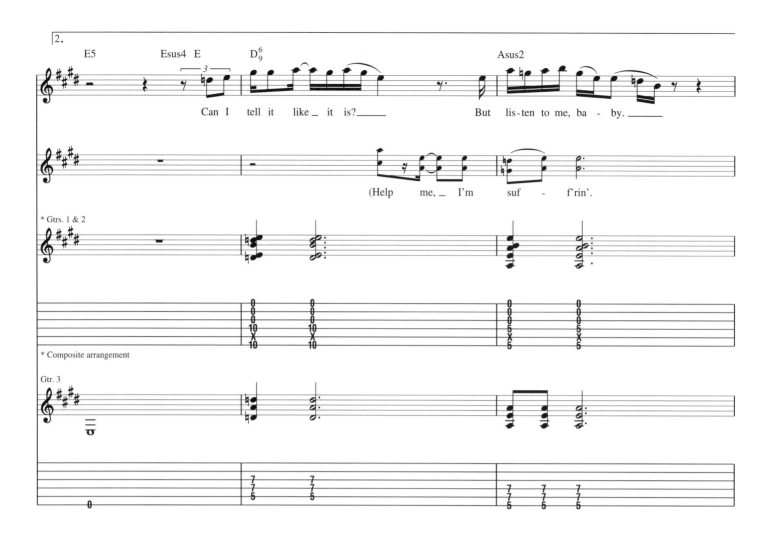

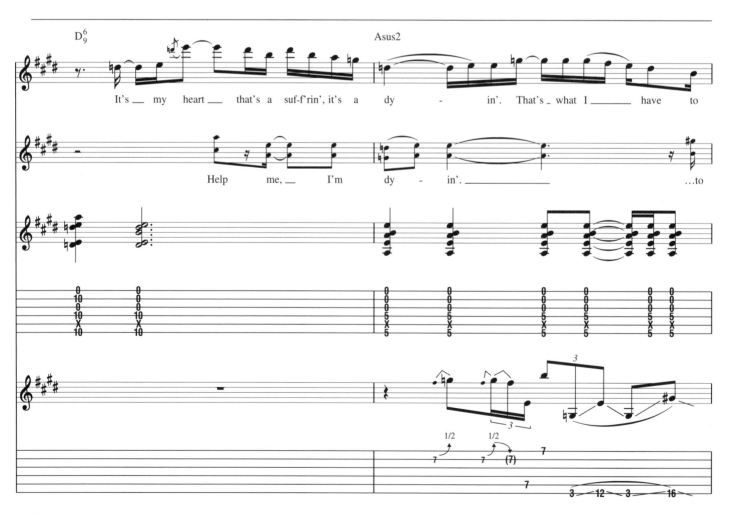

Verse

5. Chest - nut brown ca - nar - y, _____ ru - by throat - ed spar -
6. Voic - es of ____ the an - gels, ____ ring a - round _ the moon-

* Gtrs. 1 & 2

let ring

* Composite arrangement

2nd time, Gtrs. 1 & 2: w/ Rhy. Fill 3

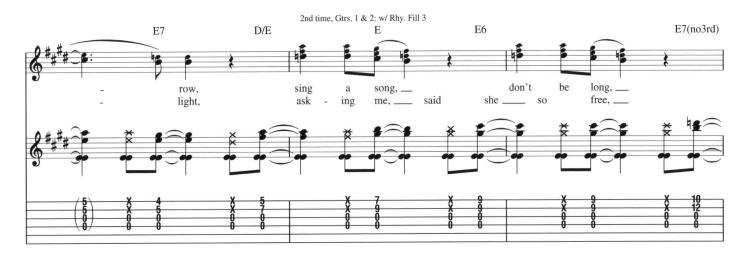

- row, sing a song, ___ don't be long, ___
- light, ask - ing me, ___ said she ___ so free, ___

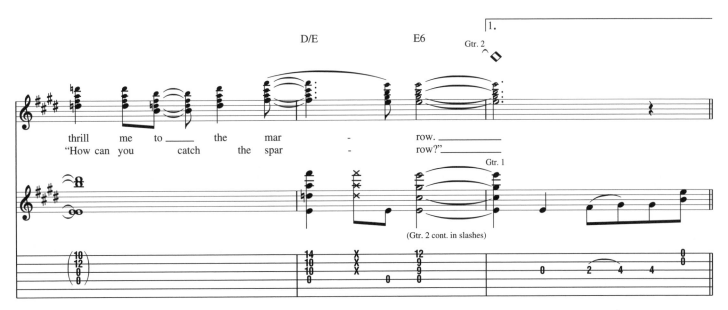

thrill me to ___ the mar - row.
"How can you catch the spar - row?" ___

(Gtr. 2 cont. in slashes)

Rhy. Fill 3
Gtrs. 1 & 2

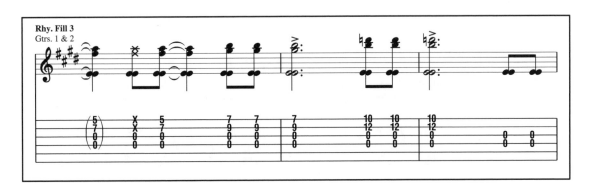

Guitar Solo

let ring ⌐ *let ring simile*

(cont. in notation)

* Hit body of gtr.

2.

Guitar Solo

E5

Gtr. 2

Gtr. 1

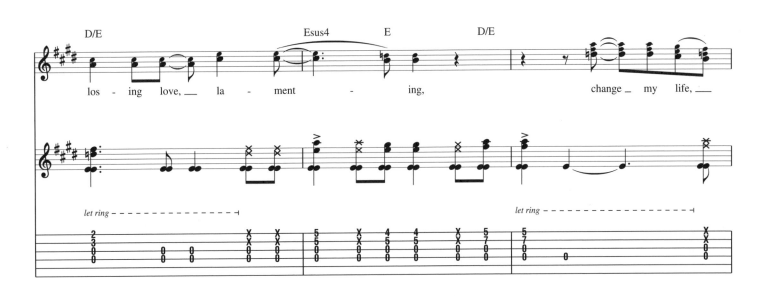

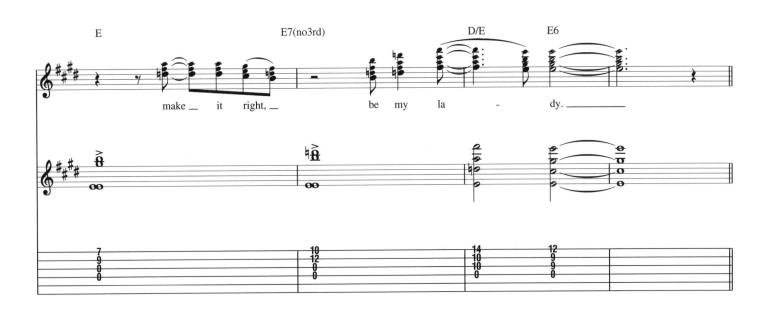

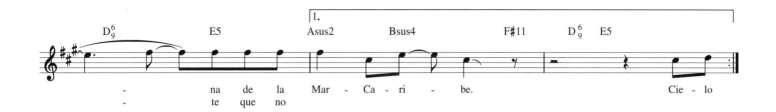

-na de la Mar - Ca - ri - be.   Cie - lo
-te que no

pue - do va - ya.   Oh, ___ va! Oh, va!   Do, do, do, do, do,   do,   do,   do, do, do, do.

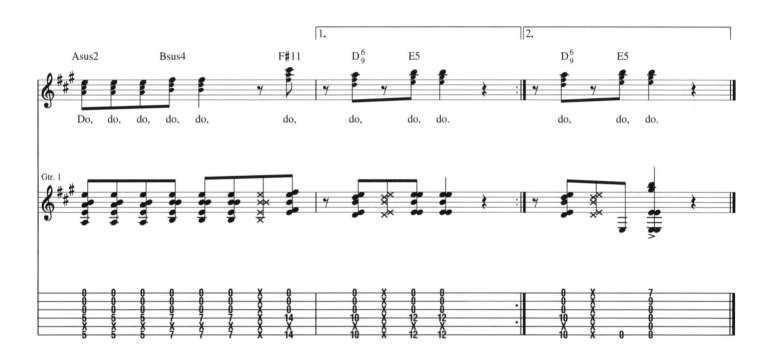

Do, do, do, do, do,   do,   do,   do, do.   do,   do,   do.

Additional Lyrics

Bridge:

3. I've got an answer,
   I'm going to fly away.
   What have I got to lose?

4. Will you come see me
   Thursdays and Saturdays? Hey, (hey,) hey.
   What have you got to lose?

Outro translation:
How happy it makes me to think of Cuba,
The smiles of the Caribbean Sea.
Sunny sky has no blood,
And how sad that I'm not able to go.
Oh, go! Oh, go!

Susie-Q

Words and Music by Dale Hawkins, Stan Lewis and Eleanor Broadwater

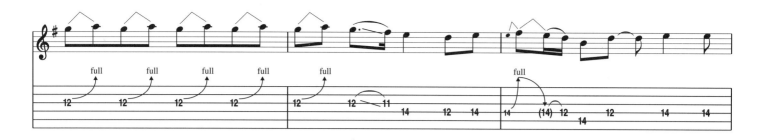

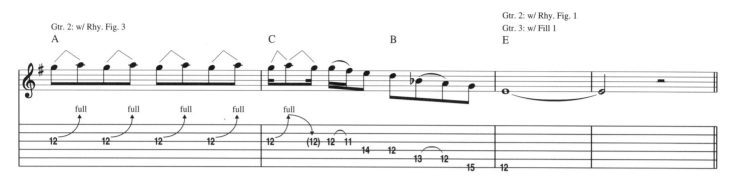

Gtr. 2: w/ Rhy. Fig. 1
Gtr. 3: w/ Fill 1

Gtr. 2: w/ Rhy. Fig. 3

D.S. al Coda 1

Interlude

Gtr. 2: w/ Rhy. Fig. 1

Em7

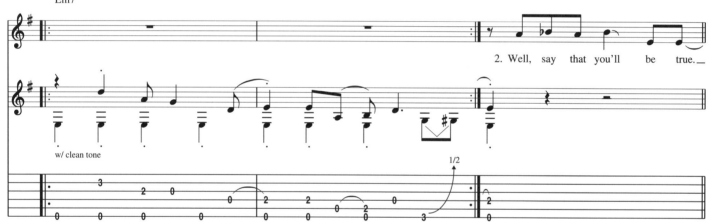

2. Well, say that you'll be true.

⊕ *Coda 1*

Guitar Solo

Gtr. 2: w/ Rhy. Fig. 1, 4 times

E

Gtr. 1

Fill 1

Gtr. 3

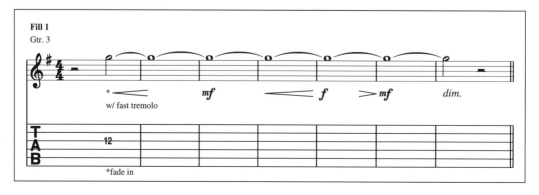

✛ Coda 2

Oh, Su - sie - Q. _____   Oh, Su - sie - Q. _____

Oh, Su - sie - Q, _____ ba - by, I love you, _____ Su - sie - Q. _____

Outro-Solo

Gtr. 2: w/ Rhy. Fig. 1, till fade, simile

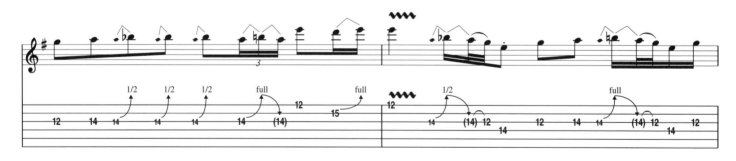

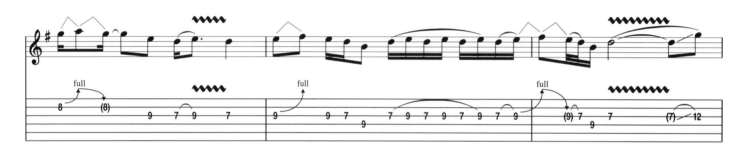

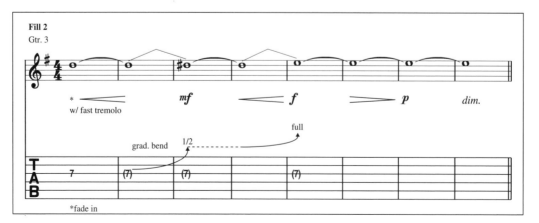

154

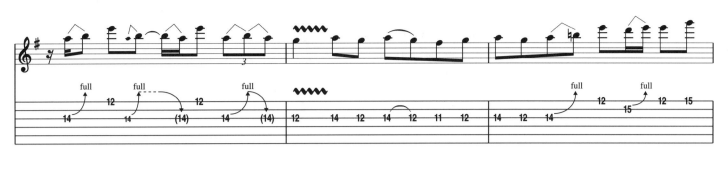

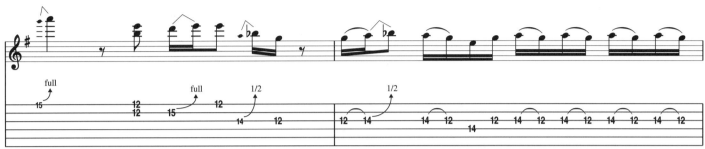

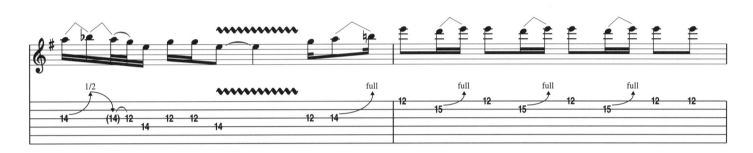

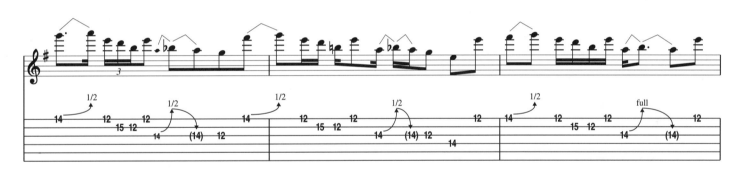

Begin Fade

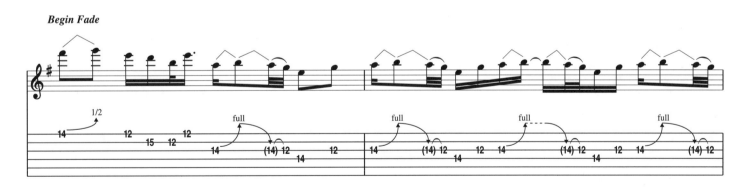

Fade Out

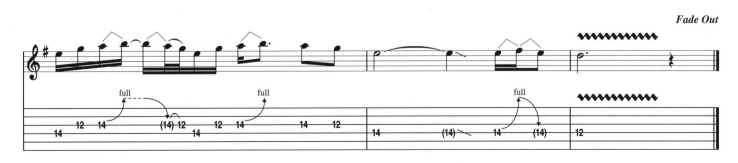

Time Is on My Side

Words and Music by Jerry Ragovoy

Recording sounds 1/4 step flat.
* Organ arr. for gtr.
** Chord symbols reflect basic harmony.

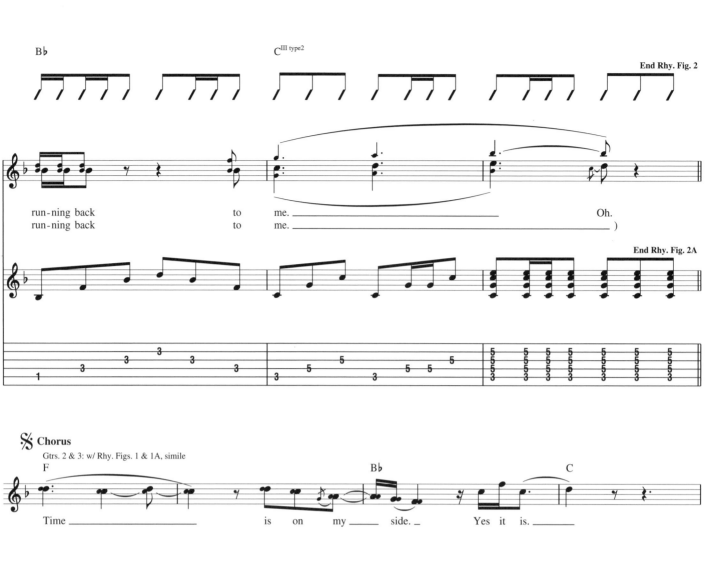

run-ning back _____ to me. _____ Oh.
run-ning back _____ to me. _____)

End Rhy. Fig. 2

End Rhy. Fig. 2A

Chorus

Gtrs. 2 & 3: w/ Rhy. Figs. 1 & 1A, simile

F   B♭   C

Time _____ is on my _____ side. Yes it is. _____

F   B♭   C

Time _____ is on my _____ side. Yes it is. _____
(Time _____ is on my _____ side. _____)

To Coda ⊕

Verse

Gtrs. 2 & 3: w/ Rhy. Figs. 2 & 2A, simile

Dm   C   Dm   G

2. You're search - ing for good times, but just wait and see.
3. 'Cause I got the real love, the kind _____ that you need.

(Oo. _____)

C   B♭   C

You'll come run - ning back. I won't have to wor - ry no more.
(You'll come run - ning back. You'll come

158

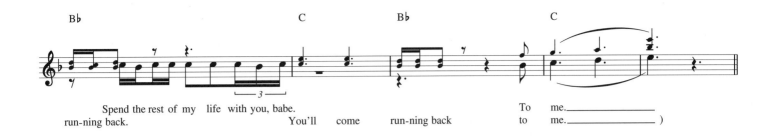

Spend the rest of my life with you, babe.
run-ning back.   You'll   come   run-ning back

To   me._____
to   me._____)

Interlude-Guitar Solo

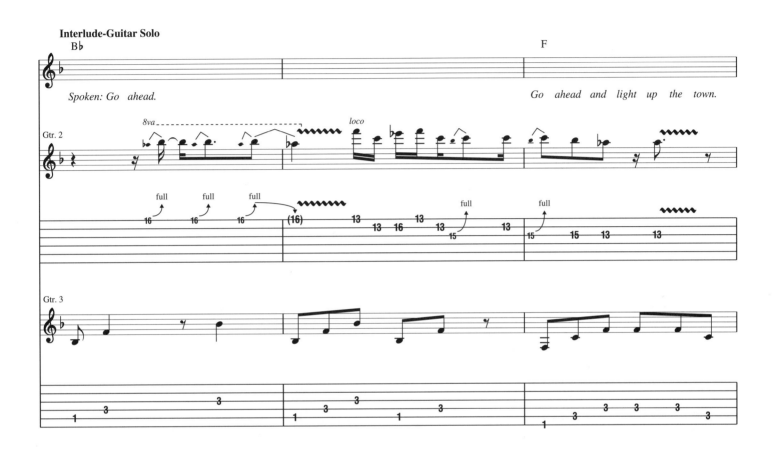

Spoken: Go ahead.

Go ahead and light up the town.

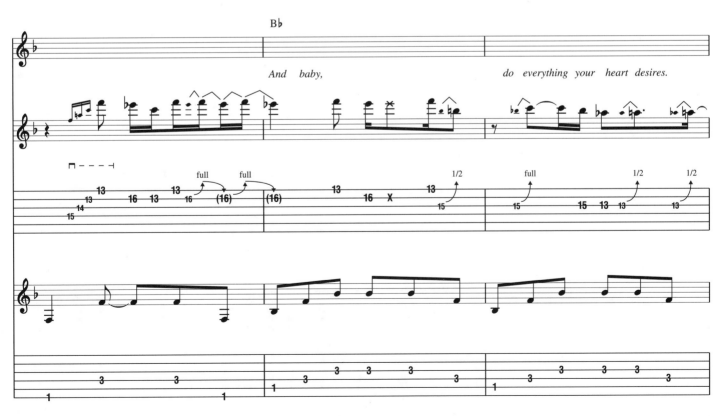

And baby,

do everything your heart desires.

(So) Tired of Waiting for You

Words and Music by Ray Davies

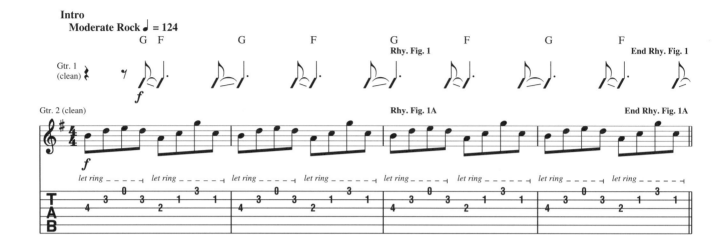

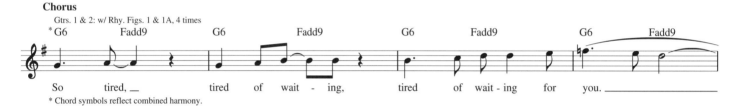

* Chord symbols reflect combined harmony.

So tired, __ tired of wait - ing, tired of wait - ing for you. __

__ So tired, __ tired of wait - ing, tired of wait - ing for

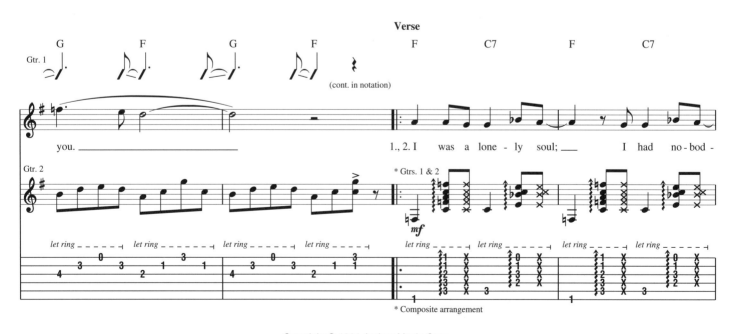

you. __

1., 2. I was a lone - ly soul; __ I had no - bod -

(cont. in notation)

* Gtrs. 1 & 2

* Composite arrangement

-y till I met you. ___ But you keep a me wait-ing all of the time.___

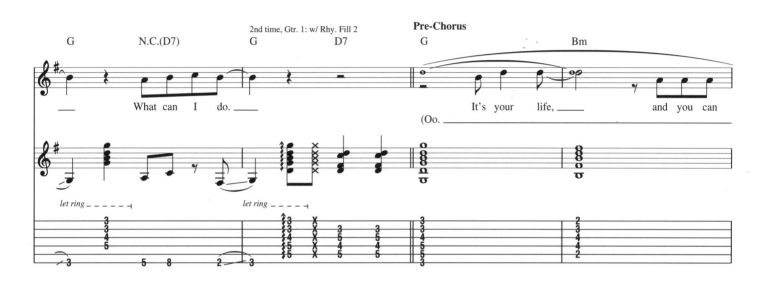

2nd time, Gtr. 1: w/ Rhy. Fill 2

Pre-Chorus

___ What can I do. ___

It's your life, ___ and you can
(Oo. ___

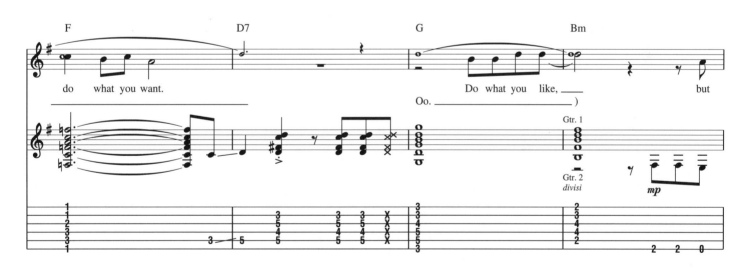

do what you want. ___

Do what you like, ___ but
Oo. ___)

Gtr. 1
Gtr. 2
divisi
mp

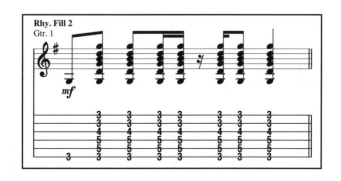

Rhy. Fill 2
Gtr. 1

mf

Train Kept A-Rollin'

Words and Music by Tiny Bradshaw, Lois Mann and Howie Kay

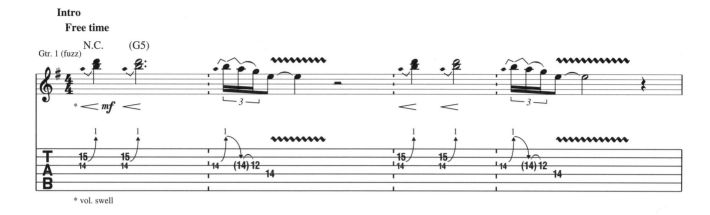

** Chord symbols reflect implied harmony.

A5   B5   A5   G5   F#5 G5

1. I'm on a

* Primary vocal

Verse

G5

train,   I met a dame.   She was a hep - ster,   well, on a rock of   fame. _ Well, she was

**Gtrs. 1 & 2

**Composite arrangement

A5   G5

pret - ty,   from New York Cit - y.   Well, then we trucked on down _ that   old ___ fair   lane; _ a with a

sweet lit-tle wom-an. Get a - long, be on your way,＿ with a heave＿

＿ and a ho,＿ ah well, I just could-n't let her go.＿ Woo!

End Riff A

End Riff A1

Guitar Solo

Walk Don't Run

By Johnny Smith

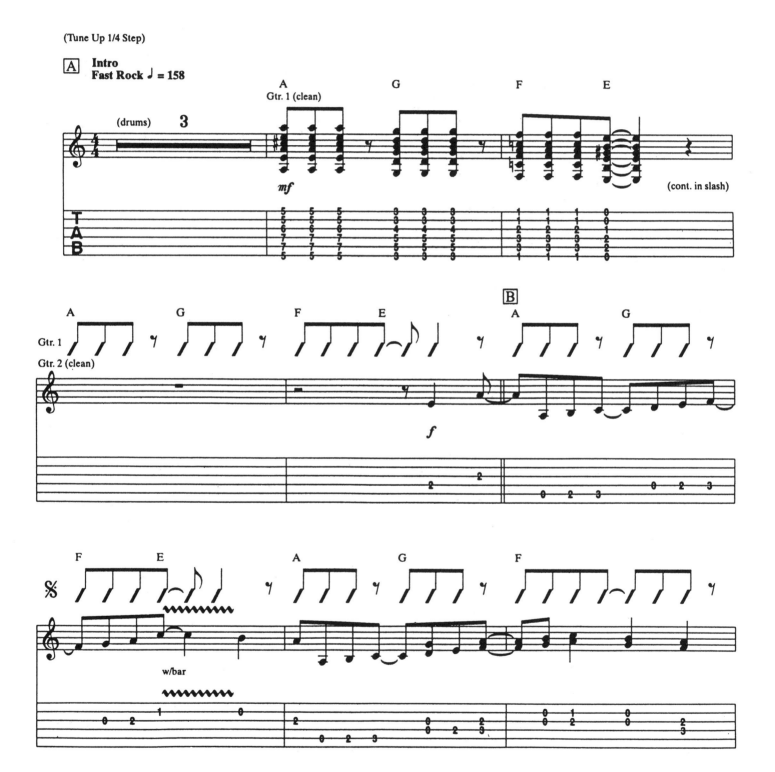

Wild Thing

Words and Music by Chip Taylor

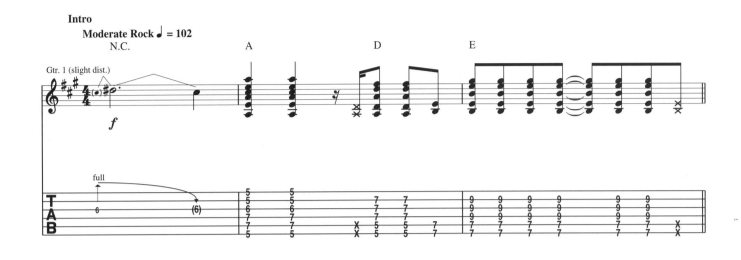

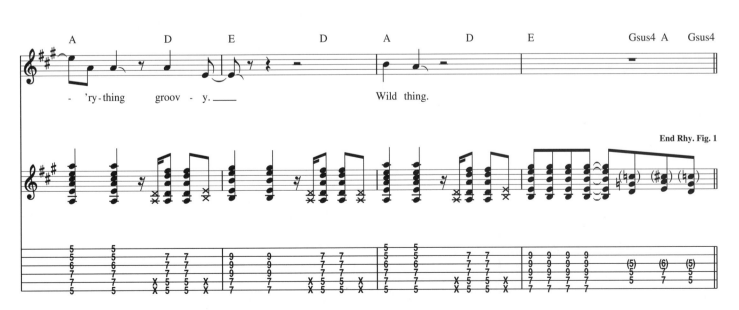

Recorder Solo

Gtr. 1: w/ Rhy. Fill 1   Gtr. 1: w/ Rhy. Fig. 1

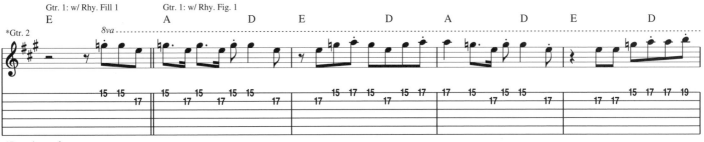

*Gtr. 2

*Recorder arr. for gtr.

D.S. al Coda

⊕ Coda

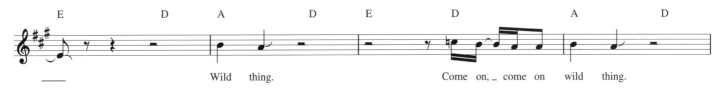

Outro-Chorus

Gtr. 1: w/ Rhy. Fig. 1, 1st 2 meas., till fade

Wild thing,   you make my heart sing.   You make ev - 'ry-thing groov - y.__

__   Wild thing.   Come on,__ come on wild thing.

Begin Fade   **Fade Out**

Shake it,__ shake it, wild thing.   I love __ you, wild thing.

Rhy. Fill 1

Gtr. 1

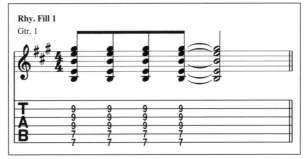

Guitar Notation Legend

Guitar Music can be notated three different ways: on a *musical staff*, in *tablature*, and in *rhythm slashes*.

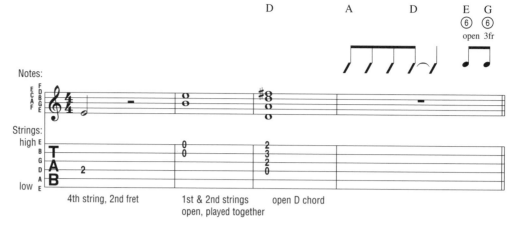

RHYTHM SLASHES are written above the staff. Strum chords in the rhythm indicated. Use the chord diagrams found at the top of the first page of the transcription for the appropriate chord voicings. Round noteheads indicate single notes.

THE MUSICAL STAFF shows pitches and rhythms and is divided by bar lines into measures. Pitches are named after the first seven letters of the alphabet.

TABLATURE graphically represents the guitar fingerboard. Each horizontal line represents a a string, and each number represents a fret.

4th string, 2nd fret

1st & 2nd strings open, played together

open D chord

Definitions for Special Guitar Notation

HALF-STEP BEND: Strike the note and bend up 1/2 step.

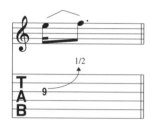

WHOLE-STEP BEND: Strike the note and bend up one step.

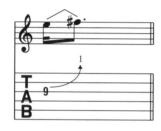

GRACE NOTE BEND: Strike the note and immediately bend up as indicated.

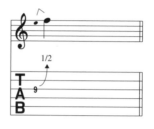

SLIGHT (MICROTONE) BEND: Strike the note and bend up 1/4 step.

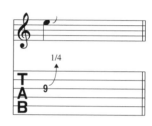

BEND AND RELEASE: Strike the note and bend up as indicated, then release back to the original note. Only the first note is struck.

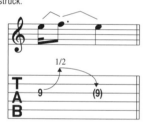

PRE-BEND: Bend the note as indicated, then strike it.

PRE-BEND AND RELEASE: Bend the note as indicated. Strike it and release the bend back to the original note.

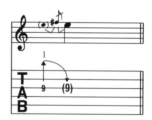

UNISON BEND: Strike the two notes simultaneously and bend the lower note up to the pitch of the higher.

VIBRATO: The string is vibrated by rapidly bending and releasing the note with the fretting hand.

WIDE VIBRATO: The pitch is varied to a greater degree by vibrating with the fretting hand.

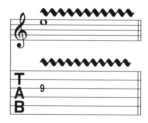

HAMMER-ON: Strike the first (lower) note with one finger, then sound the higher note (on the same string) with another finger by fretting it without picking.

PULL-OFF: Place both fingers on the notes to be sounded. Strike the first note and without picking, pull the finger off to sound the second (lower) note.

LEGATO SLIDE: Strike the first note and then slide the same fret-hand finger up or down to the second note. The second note is not struck.

SHIFT SLIDE: Same as legato slide, except the second note is struck.

TRILL: Very rapidly alternate between the notes indicated by continuously hammering on and pulling off.

TAPPING: Hammer ("tap") the fret indicated with the pick-hand index or middle finger and pull off to the note fretted by the fret hand.

NATURAL HARMONIC: Strike the note while the fret-hand lightly touches the string directly over the fret indicated.

PINCH HARMONIC: The note is fretted normally and a harmonic is produced by adding the edge of the thumb or the tip of the index finger of the pick hand to the normal pick attack.

HARP HARMONIC: The note is fretted normally and a harmonic is produced by gently resting the pick hand's index finger directly above the indicated fret (in parentheses) while the pick hand's thumb or pick assists by plucking the appropriate string.

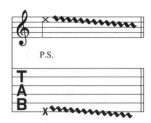

PICK SCRAPE: The edge of the pick is rubbed down (or up) the string, producing a scratchy sound.

MUFFLED STRINGS: A percussive sound is produced by laying the fret hand across the string(s) without depressing, and striking them with the pick hand.

PALM MUTING: The note is partially muted by the pick hand lightly touching the string(s) just before the bridge.

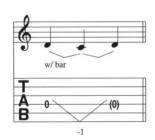

RAKE: Drag the pick across the strings indicated with a single motion.

TREMOLO PICKING: The note is picked as rapidly and continuously as possible.

ARPEGGIATE: Play the notes of the chord indicated by quickly rolling them from bottom to top.

VIBRATO BAR DIVE AND RETURN: The pitch of the note or chord is dropped a specified number of steps (in rhythm) then returned to the original pitch.

VIBRATO BAR SCOOP: Depress the bar just before striking the note, then quickly release the bar.

VIBRATO BAR DIP: Strike the note and then immediately drop a specified number of steps, then release back to the original pitch.

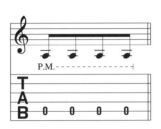

Additional Musical Definitions

>	*(accent)*	• Accentuate note (play it louder)
^	*(accent)*	• Accentuate note with great intensity
•	*(staccato)*	• Play the note short
⊓		• Downstroke
V		• Upstroke
D.S. al Coda		• Go back to the sign (𝄋), then play until the measure marked "**To Coda**," then skip to the section labelled "**Coda**."
D.C. al Fine		• Go back to the beginning of the song and play until the measure marked "***Fine***" (end).

Rhy. Fig. • Label used to recall a recurring accompaniment pattern (usually chordal).

Riff • Label used to recall composed, melodic lines (usually single notes) which recur.

Fill • Label used to identify a brief melodic figure which is to be inserted into the arrangement.

Rhy. Fill • A chordal version of a Fill.

tacet • Instrument is silent (drops out).

• Repeat measures between signs.

• When a repeated section has different endings, play the first ending only the first time and the second ending only the second time.

NOTE: Tablature numbers in parentheses mean:
1. The note is being sustained over a system (note in standard notation is tied), or
2. The note is sustained, but a new articulation (such as a hammer-on, pull-off, slide or vibrato begins), or
3. The note is a barely audible "ghost" note (note in standard notation is also in parentheses).

THE DECADE SERIES

These collections, especially for guitarists, feature the top tunes that shaped a decade, transcribed note-for-note.

The 1950s

35 pivotal songs from the early rock years: All Shook Up • Be-Bop-a-Lula • Bo Diddley • Boppin' the Blues • Cannonball • Donna • Foggy Mountain Breakdown • Get Rhythm • Guitar Boogie Shuffle • Heartbreak Hotel • Hound Dog • I'm Lookin' for Someone to Love • I'm Movin' On • I'm Your Hoochie Coochie Man • Lonesome Town • Matchbox • Moonlight in Vermont • My Babe • Poor Little Fool • Put Your Cat Clothes On • Race With the Devil • Rebel 'Rouser • Reconsider Baby • Rock Around the Clock • Rocket '88 • Rockin' Robin • Sleepwalk • Slippin' and Slidin' • Susie-Q • Sweet Little Angel • Tequila • (They Call It) Stormy Monday (Stormy Monday Blues) • Wake Up Little Susie • The World Is Waiting for the Sunrise • Yankee Doodle Dixie

_____00690543 Guitar Recorded Versions $14.95

The 1960s

30 songs that defined the '60s: Badge • Blackbird • Fun, Fun, Fun • Gloria • Good Lovin' • Green Onions • Happy Together • Hello Mary Lou • Hey Joe • Hush • I Can See for Miles • I Feel Fine • I Get Around • In the Midnight Hour • Jingo (Jin-Go-Lo-Ba) • Let's Live for Today • Louie, Louie • My Girl • Oh, Pretty Woman • On the Road Again • The Promised Land • Somebody to Love • Soul Man • Suite: Judy Blue Eyes • Susie-Q • Time Is on My Side • (So) Tired of Waiting for You • Train Kept A-Rollin' • Walk Don't Run • Wild Thing

_____00690542 Guitar Recorded Versions $14.95

The 1970s

30 top songs from the '70s: Barracuda • Best of My Love • Blue Collar Man (Long Nights) • Breakdown • Burning Love • Dust in the Wind • Evil Woman • Freeway Jam • Godzilla • Happy • Landslide • Lay Down Sally • Let It Be • Maggie May • No Woman No Cry • Oye Como Va • Paranoid • Rock and Roll Hoochie Koo • Show Me the Way • Smoke on the Water • So Into You • Space Oddity • Stayin' Alive • Teach Your Children • Time in a Bottle • Walk This Way • Wheel in the Sky • You Ain't Seen Nothin' Yet • You Really Got Me • You've Got a Friend

_____00690541 Guitar Recorded Versions $15.95

The 1980s

30 songs that best represent the decade: Caught Up in You • Down Boys • 867-5309/Jenny • Every Breath You Take • Eye of the Tiger • Fight for Your Right (To Party) • Heart and Soul • Hit Me With Your Best Shot • I Love Rock 'N Roll • In and Out of Love • La Bamba • Land of Confusion • Love Struck Baby • (Bang Your Head) Metal Health • Money for Nothing • Mony, Mony • Rag Doll • Refugee • R.O.C.K. in the U.S.A. (A Salute to '60s Rock) • Rock Me • Rock You Like a Hurricane • Running on Faith • Seventeen • Start Me Up • Summer of '69 • Sweet Child O' Mine • Wait • What I Like About You • Working for the Weekend • You May Be Right

_____00690540 Guitar Recorded Versions $15.95

The 1990s

30 essential '90s classics: All I Wanna Do • Are You Gonna Go My Way • Barely Breathing • Blue on Black • Boot Scootin' Boogie • Building a Mystery • Bulls on Parade • Come Out and Play • Cryin' • (Everything I Do) I Do It for You • Fields of Gold • Free As a Bird • Friends in Low Places • Give Me One Reason • Hold My Hand • I Can't Dance • I'm the Only One • The Impression That I Get • Iris • Jump, Jive an' Wail • More Than Words • Santa Monica • Semi-Charmed Life • Silent Lucidity • Smells Like Teen Spirit • Smooth • Tears in Heaven • Two Princes • Under the Bridge • Wonderwall

_____00690539 Guitar Recorded Versions $15.95

FOR MORE INFORMATION, SEE YOUR LOCAL MUSIC DEALER,
OR WRITE TO:

HAL•LEONARD®
CORPORATION

7777 W. BLUEMOUND RD. P.O. BOX 13819 MILWAUKEE, WI 53213

Prices, contents and availability subject to change without notice.

www.halleonard.com

RECORDED VERSIONS
The Best Note-For-Note Transcriptions Available

RECORDED VERSIONS GUITAR

ALL BOOKS INCLUDE TABLATURE

GUITAR BIBLES

from

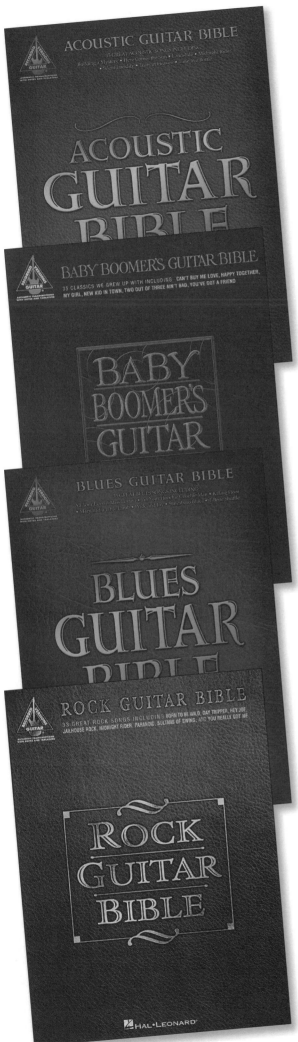

HAL•LEONARD®

Hal Leonard proudly presents the Guitar Bible series. Each volume contains best-selling songs in authentic, note-for-note transcriptions with notes and tablature. $19.95 each

ACOUSTIC GUITAR BIBLE

35 essential classics for those who prefer acoustic guitar. Songs include: Angie • Building a Mystery • Change the World • Dust in the Wind • Here Comes the Sun • Hold My Hand • Iris • Leaving on a Jet Plane • Maggie May • The Man Who Sold the World • Southern Cross • Tears in Heaven • Wild World • You Were Meant for Me • and more.
_____00690432

BABY BOOMER'S GUITAR BIBLE

Note-for-note transcriptions for 35 crown-jewel classics from rock 'n' roll's greatest era. Includes: Angie • Can't Buy Me Love • Happy Together • Hey Jude • I Heard It Through the Grapevine • Imagine • It's Still Rock and Roll to Me • Laughing • Longer • My Girl • New Kid in Town • Rebel, Rebel • Two Out of Three Ain't Bad • Wild Thing • Wonderful Tonight • and more.
_____00690412

BLUES GUITAR BIBLE

The only book of the blues you need. 35 exact transcriptions of such classics as: All Your Love (I Miss Loving) • Boom Boom • Everyday (I Have the Blues) • Hide Away • I Can't Quit You Baby • I'm Your Hoochie Coochie Man • Killing Floor • Kind Hearted Woman Blues • Mary Had a Little Lamb • Pride and Joy • Sweet Little Angel • The Things That I Used to Do • The Thrill Is Gone • and more.
_____00690437

BLUES-ROCK GUITAR BIBLE

The definitive collection of 35 note-for-note guitar transcriptions, including: Bad Love • Black Hearted Woman • Blue on Black • Boom Boom (Out Go the Lights) • Couldn't Stand the Weather • Cross Road Blues (Crossroads) • Hide Away • The House Is Rockin' • Killing Floor • Love Struck Baby • Move It on Over • Piece of My Heart • Statesboro Blues • Still Got the Blues • Train Kept a Rollin' • You Shook Me • and more.
_____00690450

COUNTRY GUITAR BIBLE

35 revered country classics in one hefty collection, including: Ain't Goin' Down ('Til the Sun Comes Up) • Blue Eyes Crying in the Rain • Boot Scootin' Boogie • Friends in Low Places • I'm So Lonesome I Could Cry • My Baby Thinks He's a Train • T-R-O-U-B-L-E • and more.
_____00690465

FOLK-ROCK GUITAR BIBLE

35 essential folk-rock guitar favorites, including: At Seventeen • Blackbird • Do You Believe in Magic • Fire and Rain • Happy Together • Here Comes the Sun • Leaving on a Jet Plane • Me and Bobby McGee • Our House • Time in a Bottle • Turn! Turn! Turn! (To Everything There Is a Season) • You've Got a Friend • and more.
_____00690464

HARD ROCK GUITAR BIBLE

The essential collection of 35 hard rock classics, including: Back in the Saddle • Ballroom Blitz • Bang a Gong (Get It On) • Barracuda • Fight the Good Fight • Hair of the Dog • Living After Midnight • Rock You like a Hurricane • School's Out • Stone Cold Crazy • War Pigs • Welcome to the Jungle • You Give Love a Bad Name • and more.
_____00690453

JAZZ GUITAR BIBLE

The one book that has all of the jazz guitar classics transcribed note-for-note, with standard notation and tablature. Includes over 30 songs: Body and Soul • Girl Talk • I'll Remember April • In a Sentimental Mood • My Funny Valentine • Nuages • Satin Doll • So What • Star Dust • Take Five • Tangerine • Yardbird Suite • and more.
_____00690466

R&B GUITAR BIBLE

A divine collection of 35 R&B classics, including: Brick House • Dancing in the Street • Fire • I Can't Help Myself (Sugar Pie, Honey Bunch) • I Got You (I Feel Good) • I Heard It Through the Grapevine • Love Rollercoaster • My Girl • Papa's Got a Brand New Bag • Shining Star • Sir Duke • Super Freak • (Your Love Keeps Lifting Me) Higher and Higher • and more.
_____00690452

ROCK GUITAR BIBLE

Exact transcriptions in notes and tab of 33 essential rock songs: All Day and All of the Night • Born to Be Wild • Day Tripper • Gloria • Hey Joe • Jailhouse Rock • Midnight Rider • Money • Paranoid • Sultans of Swing • Walk This Way • You Really Got Me • more!
_____00690313

Prices, contents, and availability subject to change without notice.

www.halleonard.com   0101